The Economics of Labour Migration

The Economics of Labour Migration

Edited by

Julien van den Broeck

Faculty of Applied Economics
University of Antwerp (RUCA)
Belgium

Edward Elgar
Cheltenham, UK - Brookfield, USA

Published by
Edward Elgar Publishing Limited
8 Landsdown Place
Cheltenham
Glos GL50 2HU
UK

Edward Elgar Publishing Company
Old Post Road
Brookfield
Vermont 05036
USA

British Library Cataloguing in Publication Data
Economics of Labour Migration
  I. Broeck, Julien Van Den
  331.127

Library of Congress Cataloguing in Publication Data
Broeck, Julien van den, 1942–
    The economics of labour migration / edited by Julien van den Broeck.
    Includes index.
    1. Alien labor—History. 2. Emigration and immigration—Economic aspects—History.
    HD6300.B76 1996
    331.6'2—dc20   95–36675
                                                                                  CIP

ISBN 1 85898 311 8

Printed and bound in Great Britain by
Biddles Limited, Guildford and King's Lynn

Contents

v

Figures

Tables

Contributors

Vernon M. Briggs, Jr.
Professor of Labor Economics, New York State School of Labor and Industrial Relations, Cornell University, New York, US.

Bimal Ghosh
Senior Consultant, International Organization for Migration and United Nations, Geneva, Switzerland; Director of the Migration and Refugees Programme, Centre for Political and Economic Analysis, Geneva, Switzerland.

Russell King
Professor of Geography, School of European Studies, University of Sussex, United Kingdom.

Julien van den Broeck
Professor of Economics, Faculty of Applied Economics, University of Antwerp (RUCA), Belgium.

Heinz Werner
Senior Research Officer, Institute for Employment Research, Bundesanstalt für Arbeit, Nuremberg, Germany.

Acknowledgements

The editor of this publication and chairman of the Conference on Labour Migration of the Belgian-Dutch Association of Post-Keynesian Studies acknowledges the financial and logistic support of the Minister-President of the Flemish Government, the Flemish Minister of Economics, SME, Scientific Policy, Energy and External Relations; the Flemish Minister of Employment and Social Affairs, Belgium; the European Commission; the National Lottery of Belgium; and the University of Antwerp (RUCA). Without their support this publication would have been impossible to realize.

Also many thanks to the authors for following editorial requests and meeting deadlines.

The help of Gis Declerck and Veerle Emboo in reordering parts of the manuscript and turning it into a camera-ready copy is also highly appreciated.

Introduction: The Economics of Labour Migration – a Process of Survival

Julien van den Broeck

Economics can be considered as the science of the survival of human beings, and because these human beings are not living in an isolated way – like Robinson Crusoe – but mostly in a societal context, the institutional environment is very important to them. It might be suggested that the institutional framework is probably the result of past societal experiences of surviving as a community. Consequently, the understanding of social processes which probably generates new experiences – either following or changing the existing institutional framework – is of crucial importance.

In order to obtain a better understanding of how people manage to survive, many of these social processes can be reduced to the relation between population and natural resources, more precisely between population growth and natural environmental change (Wilkinson, 1973). The tension generated by both processes can be considered as the driving force behind human survival behaviour. It pushes people to react to the permanently changing situation and to design new routines – institutions – in order to solve the problems caused by the new environment. When natural resources are lacking or if the population is growing too fast and natural resources are becoming scarce, people can respond in two different ways. The first way is to reduce population pressure. The second way is to find new techniques to save natural resources or to change to new and different natural resources to ease the tension. Both ways imply a particular policy with respect to a particular kind of societal order, i.e. a society with cultural and economic institutions designed to survive as a whole or only as part of a whole. Considering these possibilities, normative aspects become very

1

important when attempting to understand people's actions *vis-à-vis* their way of surviving. On the one hand, it is possible to reduce the population pressure by, for instance, designing procedures for birth control, but it is also possible to ease the population pressure by promoting emigration, either voluntary or involuntary, to other places where natural resources are bountiful. On the other hand, if natural resources are abundant and there is little population pressure, immigration (forced or unforced) can ease the problem. Consequently, the phenomenon of migration, in particular labour migration, has to be considered as one of the processes which can only be fully understood in the tension between population and natural environment. This means that only a positive-normative approach is appropriate when dealing with labour migration issues, because solving the tension problem includes a normative aspect, indicating that a purely positive inquiry is completely unsatisfactory. Clearly, handling the labour migration issue this way points to a paradigm shift in the economics of labour migration, i.e. from neoclassical economics to evolutionary economics (institutional economics), the former relying on static equilibria and natural order, the latter on dynamic processes and human institutions. By putting forward the idea that economics can be considered as the science of the survival of human beings and knowing that labour migration forms part of economics and thus of the survival process, an attempt has been made to analyse the labour migration phenomenon within an overall analytical framework. This paradigmatic approach, which can be designated as theoretically non-*ad hoc* (Mäki, 1993), prevents economists from being purely topical or thematical when dealing with the labour migration issue.

However, it cannot be denied that in the course of the development of economic theory the economics of migration has been a neglected topic. Major studies on migration issues were flagrantly missing, detracting economists from studying systematically the economic foundations, causes and consequences of migration (Passaris, 1989). It need not come as a surprise that there was no such thing as an overall conceptual framework to analyse labour migration. In the last decade, however, economists have become more aware of the need to create such a conceptual framework, because the impact of current immigration will be felt for many years and the migrant flow continues as strongly as before, making immigration policy a central issue in the debate about social policy (Borjas, 1994). An additional argument is that international migration, i.e. the flow of legally admitted residents and non-residents, contract labour migrants, illegal immigrants, asylum seekers and refugees, requires new ways of international cooperation because solitary action by individual countries does not make sense any more. Along with global trade, environmental degradation, drugs, terrorism and the proliferation of arms, international migration is a major problem for many countries and requires a coherent international policy (Meissner, Hormats, Walker and Ogata, 1993). Taking these observations into account a relevant paradigmatic approach becomes more and more essential.

Considering this ongoing process the Belgian-Dutch Association of Post-Keynesian Studies decided to adopt 'Labour Migration' as an appropriate theme for its 15th annual conference which was held at the University of Antwerp (RUCA), in Antwerp, Belgium on November 4, 1994. The chapters in this book offer a selection of the papers presented at this conference.

In the first contribution Russell King puts migration in a historical perspective, arguing that migration is of all times and places, and to a large extent determines the history of the world. Taking a look at the migration studies he not only notices a tension between the creation of models and theories and empirical case-studies, but also a conventional approach within the tradition of the neoclassical (marginalist) school and therefore ahistorical. With his contribution, King makes an attempt to correct this. In several steps the author analyses the historical process of labour migration, i.e. from the dawn of history to 1492; colonists, slaves and coolies: the development of the global market; across the oceans: international migration until the 1920s; Europe within and beyond: *Gastarbeiter* migration; and post-industrial migrations, economic restructuring and globalization. King's analysis leads him to conclude that labour migration is part of a complex of interconnected processes which cannot be understood fully by referring to the neoclassical paradigm only, pointing out that the analysis of labour migration must take into account the social context, and emphasizing implicitly the importance of institutions in the global survival process that is migration.

In his chapter Bimal Ghosh investigates in depth the relationship of economic migration and the sending countries. For the purpose of the analysis, he focuses on labour-surplus countries as migrant receivers and defines labour migration in a broad sense as including inter-country movements primarily caused or motivated by economic factors. The author further discusses theoretical models of migration and compares them with the realities of migration, stressing that labour migration is far more complex than implied in these deterministic theories. Ghosh continues to examine the results of the emigration process by suggesting that emigration affects the labour market and labour mobility, as well as the production system and the economy of the sending country mainly through the selection of migrants, remittance flows and return migration. He points out that the selection process itself is largely determined by the country's emigration policy and methods of recruitment. Ghosh concludes among other things that labour migration is neither a short cut to development nor a panacea for the sending countries' economic ills (e.g. structural unemployment), and that the possible benefits of emigration (e.g. improvement of human capital and remittance flows), which could be significant, should not be taken for granted.

The contribution of Vernon Briggs, Jr. highlights the effects of international migration and labour mobility on the receiving countries. He points out that all countries are, in fact, nations of immigrants but that only a few serve as receiving countries on a regular basis, taking into account, however, that natural limitations and man-made institutional barriers currently curtail the immigration flows. After discussing the causes of increasing world migration (e.g. population explosion and induced effects), the theoretical effects of immigration on receiving countries and the circumstances under which immigrants are admitted, the author analyses in greater detail several receiving regions such as North America, Western Europe, the oil-producing countries of the Near East and North Africa, and some special cases (e.g. Australia, Israel and Japan). In particular, he focuses on the efficiency in labour markets, the incorporation of equity concerns into public policy initiatives, and the effect of social policy on the receiving countries. Briggs stresses that planned immigration is limited to access, but that unplanned immigration, that is, immigration of refugees, asylum seekers and illegal immigrants, is expanding, imposing privation on the lowest segments of the population and the labour force. Taking into account that labour migration is more likely to be determined by the sending nations than by the receiving countries, he concludes among other things that the 'have' countries must address the systemic causes of distress in the sending countries and pursue more appropriate international policies than the option of expanding international labour migration itself. Implicitly, Briggs opts for a survival strategy which decreases resource scarcity in the sending countries in order to ease migration and not the other way around.

In the last chapter of this book, Heinz Werner thoroughly analyses the process of economic integration *vis-à-vis* the migration process in the European Union (EU). He makes clear that in order, to increase mobility, the legal framework of the European Union provides for freedom of movement for all persons within the Union. However, the author notices that there were and are no waves of migration between the Member States of the Union, which is largely due to the fact that trade has replaced labour migration in the course of European integration; it even appears that widening income gaps between regions within Member States contain more potential migration flows within than between states. Werner goes on to argue that declining demographic trends and continued industrialization in the outlying member countries of the European Union themselves will decrease the potential for labour migration within the Union, except for some categories of highly qualified manpower. According to the author the main question remains, namely, what to expect from future immigration from Eastern Europe and the Third World? He points out that considerable migration pressure will continue to exist and that actual migration will depend on whether people will perceive any improvement in their living standards in their own countries in the near future, on the rate of economic development in these countries or on possible access (illegal and legal temporary labour migration) to EU countries. The latter leads Werner to outline a European immigration policy because so far immigration policy has been regarded as a national issue, but he concludes and deplores that in spite of the involvement of the European Commission in all the work on asylum and immigration policy, national regulations and national interests are too diverse to expect a comprehensive common immigration policy in the near future.

REFERENCES

Borjas, G.J. (1994), 'The Economics of Immigration', *Journal of Economic Literature*, 32, December, pp. 1667–1717.

Mäki, U. (1993), 'Economics with Institutions – Agenda for Methodo-logical Enquiry', in U. Mäki, B. Gustafsson and C. Knudsen (eds), *Rationality, Institutions and Economic Methodology*, London and New York: Routledge, pp. 3–42.

Meissner D.M., R.D. Hormats, A.G. Walker and S. Ogata (1993), *International Migration Challenges in a New Era*, Report to the Trilateral Commission No 44, New York, Paris and Tokyo: The Trilateral Commission.

Passaris, C. (1989), 'Immigration and the Evolution of Economic Theory', *International Migration*, 27 (4), December, pp. 525–41.

Wilkinson, R.G. (1973), *Poverty and Progress – An Ecological Model of Economic Development*, London: Methuen.

1 Migration in a World Historical Perspective

Russell King

INTRODUCTION

To write a chapter on the history of migration is a bit like trying to squeeze an ocean into a test-tube. This watery analogy is quite appropriate since migrants are often portrayed as travelling in waves, currents, flows, even floods. But the real problem is the ubiquity and diversity of migratory phenomena throughout history. To a large extent the history of the world *is* migration: conquest, imperialism, colonization and capitalism often involve mass movements of people in settlement, flight, displacement, attraction or repulsion.

A sampling of even a small portion of migration's vast literature reveals a tension between attempts to create models and theories on the one hand, and the numerous empirical case-studies which tend to emphasize unique circumstances on the other. The case-studies are nearly always interesting but have limited theoretical validity or general application; the theories either state the obvious or involve unrealistic assumptions. Universal propositions offered to 'explain' migration, such as its link to the development of the international economy or the desire of individuals to improve their economic and social conditions, are true but trite. As Baines (1991, p. 74) points out, they could apply to almost any aspect of human behaviour. On the other hand, it is perhaps precisely *because* it is so difficult to make generalizations about migration that it is such an important and fascinating subject to study!

The historical literature on migration is extensive but uneven. Most has been written about slave migrations, immigration to North

America during the 'great age' of transatlantic migration in the 19th and early 20th centuries, and postwar labour migration in Western Europe. These literatures span many languages, genres and points of view. In trying to skim the best of these writings, I offer what is inevitably a personal interpretation of the history of migration. My main concentration will be on labour migration, but not exclusively. It is important to see how labour migration is historically and socially embedded in wider migration processes. Labour migration, in any case, can be either broadly or narrowly defined. A narrow definition would focus on the specific recruitment of foreign workers by higher-order authorities such as governments or employers; or it might focus on the individual migrant's desire to find work abroad. A broader definition would recognize that many other types of migration – family migration, refugee movements, brain drain etc. – contain people who sooner or later will be seeking work and will therefore have impacts on the labour market.

In their introductory overview of a collection of essays on the history of labour migration, Marks and Richardson (1984) examine the value of existing historical studies on the theme. A certain ambivalence is evident. On the one hand it is pointed out that historical studies tend to be parochial and over-long on factual detail; on the other it is maintained that 'only through a theoretically-informed and historically specific approach can a more comprehensive and satisfactory account of labour migration be produced'. But there is a deeper problem to be tackled. According to Marks and Richardson (1984, pp. 3–6) the conventional approach to the study of migrant labour is carried out within the marginalist school of economics and is based on the assumption that the factors of production are given *a priori*. Such an approach 'explains' labour migration in terms of an oversupply acting as a 'natural mechanism' working in everyone's best interest to restore some kind of notional 'balance'. This ahistorical approach to demography divorces migration from questions of economic strategy and the social relations of production. Above all, it does not say anything about who *controls* migration, nor about limitations on individual migrants' freedom and choices. Most studies of labour migration barely touch on the extent to which individual migrants are aware of the structural conditions which surround their apparently free-willed actions. Even sophisticated social surveys which elicit and explore lists of reasons from migrants for their movement can hardly be considered a satisfactory explanation for why migration takes place. This point can be taken even further by arguing that the study of migration is in fact the study of structural transformations by which economies and societies are made and remade. In this way the 'economic' aspect of labour migration cannot be hived off from the political and the social: all are part of the same phenomenon.

This chapter follows a broadly historical treatment by examining the evolution of migration through a series of 'historical types'. After a brief description of ancient migrations, attention is mainly given to slave and indenture migrations, the transoceanic settler migrations of the 19th century, the postwar labour migrations which affected Western Europe, North America and other poles of the global economy during the 1950s, 1960s and 1970s, and finally the post-industrial migrations of the 1980s and 1990s. Most of the analysis is of international migration. Internal or intra-national migrations cannot be included because of space limitations: although they often overlap or run parallel to international movements, they are normally of a different qualitative character and occur across more limited geographical scales except within very large countries such as the United States or China.

FROM THE DAWN OF HISTORY TO 1492

Migrations have been part of human history since the dawn of time. It has been claimed that the tendency to migrate is innate and one of the distinguishing features of *homo sapiens* (Du Toit and Safa, 1975, p. 1). In an interesting essay on the history of human migration, William McNeill (1978) stresses that 'roving behaviour' has had a crucially important role in human evolution: humankind could not have become the dominant globe-girding species that it has without the roving instinct and the more consolidated migrations that followed such exploratory behaviour. Interestingly migration lies at the heart of a major debate on the origins of human life on earth. This is the debate between those who believe that *homo sapiens* evolved independently in different parts of the globe – Africa, Asia, Europe (but not the Americas) – and those who believe that early humans developed first in East Africa and radiated out from there to colonize the rest of the world (Fagan, 1990). Less controversial is the fact that, in a sense, all Americans are migrants. Even before the arrival of Europeans, the Indians (or native Americans) had migrated from Asia, travelling down from Alaska to Tierra del Fuego.

Of course, such early migrations can hardly be labelled labour migrations, but if we fast-forward in time to the rise of urban civilizations in the Middle East and start to look at the way cities and imperial powers used labour, we do begin to see parallels and regularities emerging. We see, for instance, labour being forced or encouraged to migrate from countryside to town, from overpopulated to underpopulated areas, or from recently-conquered territories to the colonial metropole or to another part of the empire. McNeill (1978) has advanced the thesis that virtually throughout civilized history from Sumerian times until the 19th century, four migration currents can be distinguished. These four migration types are identified by a double distinction, first by class into peasants and elites, and second by direction – inwards towards the cities and outwards towards the frontier. Figure 1.1 provides a schematic representation of the four types.

The mass migration of peasants and proletarians obviously represents the closest approximation to modern labour migrations, although McNeill's model is driven by considerations of demography and especially mortality rather than explicit recognition of the factor of labour demand. McNeill believes that, ever since their original development, cities have failed to reproduce their populations because of high mortality or 'endemic die-off' caused by urban diseases which fed off dense concentrations of people. He cites evidence from ancient Mesopotamia and 18th-century London (where an annual immigration of 6,000 persons was necessary simply to maintain the population) to support his case. Hence rural migrants beat a path to the city not only to improve themselves, but also to replenish the city's demographic reservoir and labour reserves.

The second traditional migration current for rural peasants ran in the opposite direction, towards the frontier of settlement or colonization. Lands towards the periphery of city-states or urban-centred empires were continually being made available by conquest and by disease. This phenomenon is again traceable to the remote past but its most well-known examples are in the Americas and the Tropics where Europeans regularly decimated native populations by mowing them down with new diseases – a kind of 'death by migration' (Curtin, 1989). Both empty and newly-depopulated frontier zones thus became available for pioneer settlement from overcrowded rural regions belonging to the metropolitan power.

Elite migrations have been less important quantitatively than peasant migrations but their role in shaping world events and in paving the way for subsequent waves of mass migration should not be under-estimated. Once again, they have flowed in two main directions (Figure 1.1). First, as traders, missionaries, administrators and colonizers, elites migrated outwards from the urban centres towards the peripheries – a centrifugal movement observable since the megalithic builders migrated through the Mediterranean and around the coasts of western Europe to the Baltic Sea. Second there was an inward move towards the centre as empires were invaded by barbarian tribes originating from the periphery. According to McNeill, the early political history of Eurasia is largely made up of successive waves of barbarian raiders coming in off the steppes and deserts of Central Asia and the Middle East.

Some of McNeill's examples of migration have parallels in modern migrations, others do not. Population displacement by conquest and epidemic have painful echoes in the very recent policies of genocide and ethnic cleansing in Rwanda and the former Yugoslavia. The long-standing problems of the exhaustion of food supplies in relation to given levels of agricultural technology and population density are familiar to us in the recent history of Sahelian Africa, where the situation is further complicated by war and political factors. McNeill's two basic distinctions between peasant and elite migration, and between city-ward migration and migration to the frontier, are also highly relevant to modern migrations, as we shall see. I tend to feel that his emphasis on mortality and epidemics as migration factors is overstressed, but again there are later historical parallels to be drawn.

From this general consideration of McNeill's model of historical migration types, I move to a more concrete account of the migrations that pre-dated the emergence of the world capitalist system after the 16th century. Naturally there were many significant migrations in different parts of the world. Only a few important examples can be

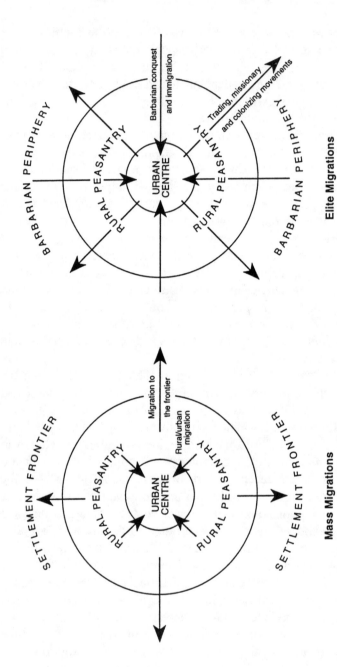

Barbarian conquest
and immigration

Trading, missionary
and colonizing movements

BARBARIAN PERIPHERY

RURAL PEASANTRY

URBAN
CENTRE

RURAL PEASANTRY

BARBARIAN PERIPHERY

Elite Migrations

Migration to
the frontier

SETTLEMENT FRONTIER

RURAL PEASANTRY

Rural/urban
migration

URBAN
CENTRE

RURAL PEASANTRY

SETTLEMENT FRONTIER

Mass Migrations

Source: McNeill, 1978, pp. 9, 11.

Figure 1.1   A model of early migrations

mentioned; these are drawn mainly from Segal (1993, pp. 8–11). Those selected are chosen partly on the criterion of having left a permanent historical legacy, and partly to demonstrate historical antecedence in the ways in which migration was subsequently used as a tool for economic and political strategy.

Figure 1.2 shows that the main pre-1500 long-range migrations have a particular clustering around the Mediterranean, cradle of Old-World civilization. Migration in ancient Greece was closely linked to colonial policy. Between 950 and 800 BC the Greeks founded colonies throughout the eastern Mediterranean and in southern Italy. Further thrusts to Marseilles and the coast of Spain consolidated a Greek fringe round much of the Mediterranean. By the 5th century BC, Athens was selling off the people of captured cities as slaves and replacing them with Greek colonists. Under Rome the establishment of colonies throughout the Mediterranean between 140 BC and AD 640 was followed initially by the freeing and enfranchisement of slaves; later, under the Empire, commercial slavery and the transport of slaves became big business.

Thus already in the classical era labour was recruited by the transport and enslavement of conquered peoples who functioned as auxiliary reservoirs of labour for the imperial power. Thousands of slaves were moved to mines, public works projects and agricultural estates. The Egyptians, the Arabs and the Ottoman Turks were likewise capable of transporting large numbers of prisoners of war to distant centres. Slave raids as far afield as East Africa brought additional manpower for tasks for which local labour was insufficient or unwilling. Slave soldieries, household slaves and slave cultivators were all common before 1500. Since slaves rarely were allowed to reproduce themselves, all three kinds of slaves depended on the supply of enslavable people somewhere at a distance.

Around the south of the Mediterranean the expansion of Islam from the holy cities of Mecca and Medina as far as Spain took place between 640 and 1250 via a combination of migration, settlement, conquest, conversion, intermarriage and slavery. This remarkable long-distance religious migration was probably the most significant of those marked on Figure 1.2, although this statement is perhaps unfair to the major role that migrations have played throughout Chinese history – according to Lee (1978) the planned rural migrations of the

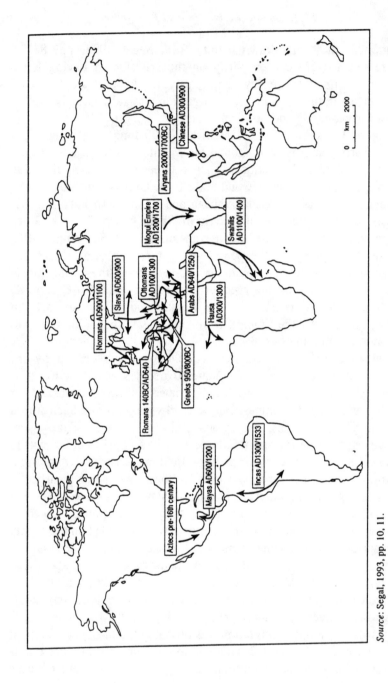

Source: Segal, 1993, pp. 10, 11.

Figure 1.2   Long-range migrations prior to 1500

3rd century BC, the widespread migrations of the 4th century AD and the sustained southward pioneer migrations of the 15th century were three great periods of migration by any definition.

In Central Asia two migrations separated by more than three millennia penetrated northern India: the Aryans (2000–1700 BC) brought Sanskrit, slavery and the caste system; and invasions of central Asian muslims from the Mogul Empire (AD1200–1700) involved conquest, religious conversion to Islam, migration, settlement and the establishment of sultanates. At approximately the same time as the latter of these two Asian migrations, Africa was also affected by two Islamic migrations: the first down the east coast (AD1100––1400) with commercial and slaving ports established at Mogadishu, Dar-es-Salaam, Mombasa and elsewhere; and the second from Sudan westwards towards northern Nigeria and Lake Chad, again involving a mixture of conquest, religious conversion, migration and slavery (AD1300–1800). In Central and South America the Aztecs, Mayas and Incas were all migrating through conquest and settlement before the arrival of the Spanish.

Finally on Figure 1.2, and back again in Europe, came the great Slavic tribal migrations, between AD 600 and 900. From their homeland north of the Carpathians they fanned out in three directions: southern Slavs settled in the Balkans, founding a Christian Bulgarian kingdom, but then being partially incorporated in the westward-expanding Ottoman Empire (the legacies of these ethnic and religious migrations are still being worked out today in former Yugoslavia); the western Slavs migrated to Bohemia and Poland; and eastern Slavs settled in central Russia, trading with the Vikings. During AD 900–1100 the Vikings migrated from Scandinavia to conquer and settle Normandy, from which other invasions were launched both northwards to England in 1066, and south as far as Sicily. The legacy of the fair-haired Normans can still be seen today in the racial mix of Sicilians.

Most of these migrations hurriedly referred to above are little-documented. What is important for our purposes, however, are the conditions giving rise to such movements: overpopulation, state planning, slavery, migration for religious purposes, war etc. It is also important to realize that migration was usually part of a complex of interconnected processes such as conquest, settlement, intermarriage, religious conversion – processes which create, or change, the character of places.

COLONISTS, SLAVES AND COOLIES: THE DEVELOPMENT OF THE GLOBAL LABOUR MARKET

We now move on to a period when international migrations, both voluntary and involuntary, gathered pace. Starting with Columbus's landing in the New World in 1492, European colonization of the Americas and of other world areas completely transformed the scale and distance of international migrations. Spain's destructive colonization of the Caribbean and South America marked the first stage in the making and remaking of capitalism as a world market system in which labour, like capital and other goods, would be circulated as a commodity – but not necessarily as a freely traded commodity. In fact, under the colonial system slavery and indenture were a widespread response by both governments and individual capitalists to a situation of abundant supplies of land, the availability or potential availability of primary resources such as crops and minerals, and the impracticability of using 'free' labour. Indeed, as Corrigan (1977) stresses, in many colonial settings constraint and bondage of labour, rather than the establishment of a free market for labour, were the very basis on which capitalism developed.

The available literature on this period is quite rich, and this literature points to the complexity of labour arrangements and to the crudeness of distinctions between voluntary and involuntary migration. The form of labour migration known as indenture was subject to a particularly wide variety of practices, both at the recruiting and the receiving ends. The present brief overview will have to overlook such subtleties and concentrate on the three main types of international labour transfer under the colonial regime: settlers, slaves and indentured labourers or coolies.

First, much voluntary emigration from Europe occurred as a direct function of colonial settlement. Although reliable figures are scarce, some examples of these early colonial settler migrations were the 437,000 Spaniards who migrated to the Caribbean, Central and South America between 1506 and 1650, the 70,000 Portuguese who migrated to Brazil before 1650, the 10,000 French who settled mainly in Quebec before 1700, the 1 million British and Irish who migrated to North America by 1815, and the smaller communities of Dutch who settled in New York (originally called New Amsterdam), Capetown and Indonesia (Segal, 1993, pp. 14–15).

Not all of these 'voluntary' immigrants were free from constraints, however. A lesser-known aspect of these early colonial migrations concerns the large numbers of indentured white migrants who left their European homelands, especially England, during the 17th century. These migrants, mainly indentured servants, were given free passage across the Atlantic, board and lodging during the period of the indenture (normally four years), and some payment in land or money at the end of their indenture. Gemery (1980) estimates that 380,000 British migrants crossed the Atlantic in this way during 1630–1700, two-thirds of them to the West Indies and the rest to the North American colonies, especially Virginia and Maryland. This indenture system, like the others which followed it, was a means of securing a supply of migrant labour in the medium term; even after the onset of slavery it was still used to recruit overseers and craftsmen. The outward impetus from the home areas should not be ignored, however. Souden (1984) believes that the system was a reflection of English apprentice and domestic servant traditions, and that it was as much driven by demographic and economic push pressures in England as by the pull of labour demand in the plantation economies.

The transatlantic slave trade that started in earnest in the 17th century was preceded by the enslavement of the Indians (or native Americans) by the Spanish. According to Lydia Potts (1990) Indian slavery was the first large-scale system in the history of capitalism to exploit the workers of conquered territories outside of Europe. In terms of its scale and destructive significance, it exceeded the enslavement of the African peoples. Potts (1990, pp. 9–31) gives a harrowing account of this most tragic epoch in world population history, including some details of the migration processes associated with it. Some examples are the inter-island forced transfer of labour from the Bahamas and Lesser Antilles to work in the gold mines of Hispaniola; the large-scale movement of enslaved Indians from Nicaragua to Panama and Peru; the rotation of workers, including women, into the horrendous working conditions of the silver mines of Potosi, 4,000 metres up in the Andes; and the movement of people onto the *encomienda* estates which were a direct descendant from

Spanish feudalism (still in existence in Spain at the time). Death rates through overwork, disease and often plain slaughter were extraordinarily high. For instance, barely one-fifth survived their first year in the Potosi mines whilst of the 60,000 Indians brought from the Bahamas to Hispaniola during the decade following 1509, only 800 were still alive in 1519. Throughout the early decades of the Spanish empire, forced migration or shipment of local labourers virtually amounted to a death sentence.

More dramatic, from a strictly migrational point of view, were the great African slave migrations that ensued. The forced transport of slaves from West Africa was actually started by Portugal as early as the mid-15th century; the slaves were taken to Portugal to be house-servants. The virtual annihilation of the Indian labour force in the Spanish American colonies led to some slave migrations in the early 16th century; by 1570 the number of slaves in the Spanish colonies was 40,000, rising to 857,000 by 1650 according to one estimate (quoted by Potts, 1990, p. 31). However, the real pioneers of transatlantic slavery were not the Spanish but the Portuguese in Brazil. By about 1600 north-east Brazil had become one vast sugar plantation and this crop, together with African slave labour, was the backbone of the Brazilian colonial economy (Russel-Wood, 1982). Estimates of the number of slaves brought to Brazil before the banning of slave trading in this region range from 3 million upwards.

If slavery was pioneered and tested by the Spanish and Portuguese, it reached its most dynamic and fully developed form in the Caribbean and in the southern states of North America in the 18th and 19th centuries. By this time Spain had lost its pre-eminent position in the Caribbean and essentially retained only Cuba. The remainder of the islands and some adjacent coastal territories were shared by other European powers and especially by the British, who became the dominant power in the region and the main transporter of slaves. Britain had taken possession of Jamaica, Barbados, Trinidad, the Bahamas, Bermuda and many smaller islands. The slave states of the southern USA – Virginia, the Carolinas, Georgia, Mississippi, Alabama, Louisiana – were also originally British colonies. France took over Martinique, Guadeloupe, Haiti and French Guyana, whilst Dutch territories included Surinam and Curaçao. Once the native Indians had been wiped out, typically each Caribbean island came to contain a small group of white residents and a large number of slaves.

In the mid-1830s, for instance, Jamaica had 20,000 whites and 310,000 slaves, Antigua 2,000 whites and 29,000 slaves and Martinique 9,000 and 78,000 (Patterson, 1982).

A full account of the quantitative, historical and geographical aspects of the slave trade would take many hundreds of pages, so only a brief outline can be given here. Enslavement and transport of Africans by Europeans actually stretched over more than 400 years, from 1445 to 1870. However, the vast majority of the slave trade took place during the period 1700–1850, the period of maximum development of the sugar economy in the Caribbean islands and of the cotton plantations in the southern USA. Curtin (1969) provides a detailed breakdown both in time and geographically (Table 1.1) and comes to the conclusion that it involved the forced transfer of about 10 million Africans (other historians have estimated up to 20 million, but their work is less thorough than Curtin's).

Table 1.1 does not record the less well-known flank of African slave migration – the 4 million or so East Africans who were transported and enslaved into societies in the Persian Gulf and the Middle East, and the smaller-scale trans-Saharan slave trade. Both of these are indicated on Figure 1.3, which charts the geography of the African slave trade. The map shows that West Africa was the main area affected, this area being nearest to both Europe and America. But other areas were also tapped. During the 17th and 18th centuries Portugal, having lost ground to the British and French in West Africa, supplied Brazil with slaves from Mozambique, whilst North American ships sailed to Madagascar in an attempt to circumvent England's monopoly of West African slavery.

Slaves were obtained by various means ranging from naked hunting and capture to orderly agreements with local chiefs. Young adult males aged 15–25 years were preferred but young women and children were also transported. After capture they were assembled at rallying points on the coast or offshore islands, branded with the mark of the shipping company and jammed into ships for the crossing. Estimates of the proportions who died during the voyage ranged from 15 to 33 per cent (Potts, 1990, p. 45). In the famous 'triangular trade' slave merchants sailing out of ports like Bristol and Liverpool traded European goods (clothing, cheap jewellery, guns, spirits etc.) for slaves, took the slaves across the Atlantic where they were sold for cash, the proceeds being used to bring slave-labour plantation crops

Table 1.1   The Atlantic slave trade 1451–1870 (all data '000)

Importing region/country	1451–1600	1601––1700	1701––1810	1811––70	Total
Old World	149.9	25.1	–	–	175.0
Europe	48.8	1.2	–	–	50.0
São Tomé	76.1	23.9	–	–	100.0
Atlantic Islands	25.0	–	–	–	25.0
Spanish America	75.0	292.5	578.6	606.0	1,552.1
Brazil	50.0	560.0	1,891.4	1,145.4	3,646.8
British Caribbean	–	263.7	1,401.3	–	1,665.0
Jamaica	–	85.1	662.4	–	747.5
Barbados	–	134.5	252.5	–	387.0
Leeward Islands	–	44.1	301.9	–	346.0
Trinidad	–	–	22.4	–	22.4
Grenada	–	–	67.0	–	67.0
Other BWI	–	–	95.1	–	95.1
French Caribbean	–	155.8	1,348.4	96.0	1,600.2
Santo Domingo	–	74.6	789.7	–	864.3
Martinique	–	66.5	258.3	41.0	365.8
Guadeloupe	–	12.7	237.1	41.0	290.8
French Guiana	–	2.0	35.0	14.0	51.0
Louisiana	–	–	28.3	–	28.3
Dutch Caribbean	–	40.0	460.0	–	500.0
Danish Caribbean	–	4.0	24.0	–	28.0
British N.America	–	–	348.0	51.0	399.0
Total	274.9	1,341.1	6,051.7	1,898.4	9,566.1
Annual average	1.8	13.4	55.0	31.6	22.8

Source: Curtin, 1969, p. 268.

(sugar, coffee, rum, cotton, etc.) back to Europe.

Profits to the slave traders were high: selling prices of slaves were at least four times the prices paid in cash or in kind in Africa. Slaves were so freely available, and delivery so smooth, that worries about the longer-term reproduction of this labour could be postponed. These market conditions of strong demand but a constantly replenished supply meant that slaves were grossly ill-treated, not only on the voyage but also by plantation owners and managers who often fed, clothed and housed them to minimal standards. As a rule, slave-owners expected their slaves to be 'written-off' within five years: one-

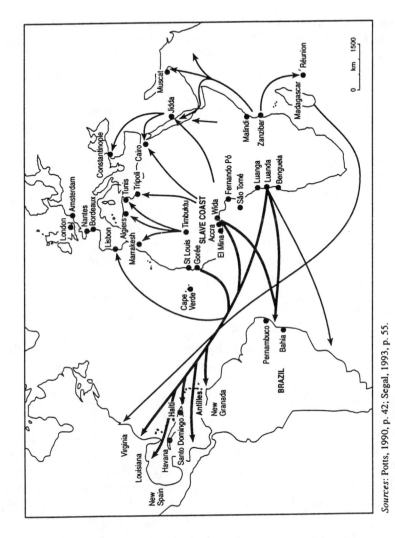

Sources: Potts, 1990, p. 42; Segal, 1993, p. 55.

Figure 1.3   The African slave trade

21

third of those imported into Jamaica died within three years (Potts,1990, p. 49).

Most slaves were deployed on plantations where they worked in gangs driven by overseers. Slave labour was the basis of commodity production in these colonies and accounted for a large measure of the prosperity enjoyed by the metropolitan powers – Britain, France, the Netherlands, Spain and Portugal. In his fine essay on Caribbean slave migration, Orlando Patterson stressed the key role played by profits from 'brown gold' (sugar) in the accumulation of commercial capital to feed the European Industrial Revolution: 'it is hard to imagine today the incredible wealth generated by these tiny islands in the eighteenth century, and the enormous role they played in the political and economic life of the major European imperial states, as well as in the development of prerevolutionary America' (Patterson, 1978, p. 107).

Prospects for 'promotion' open to slaves were very restricted. A very few were able to switch to domestic service or skilled craft work. Others took more drastic measures: the communities of escaped slaves called 'maroons' who lived in the hills of Jamaica and other larger islands were named after earlier slave escapees known as *cimarrones* in 16th-century Spanish America (the word *cimarron* means a tamed animal escaped to the wild). As Potts (1990, p. 49) rightly points out, however, these 'escape routes' for slaves 'should not blind us to the fact that the plantation economy of the Caribbean was based on the extreme attrition of human labour'.

The market conditions of slave labour obviously changed when the slave trade was outlawed in 1807. One reaction was a reshuffling of slave labour within the Caribbean. Inter-island migration took place from long-settled, overcrowded islands such as Barbados where soil exhaustion had set in to recently-acquired territories such as Trinidad and Demerara where the soil was still fertile (Eltis, 1972). Another reaction was that, throughout the Caribbean, plantation owners took greater interest in the reproduction of slave labour on the spot. Hence female slaves became more valuable and breeding was encouraged. This had always been the case in the United States where slavery as an institution developed later and with a more even balance between the sexes. Table 1.1 shows the low number of slaves destined direct for the USA – barely 400,000 or 4 per cent of the total transatlantic shipment. As early as the 18th century the USA slave population was naturally replacing itself and by the time slavery was abolished in 1865 only one in ten of the slaves living there had been born in Africa (Curtin, 1969). In fact by the 1830s some southern states like Virginia and South Carolina were actually exporting slaves and earning substantial revenues in the process. As well as plantation work, slaves in America were also used in coalmines, iron works, forestry and railway building.

The migratory significance of slaves did not stop with the abolition of slavery in the 19th century: far from it. Forced apprenticeships for freed slaves tied them to their former work-masters for 4–6 years, but soon new internal migrations took place as former slaves quit the hated plantations of the coastal lowlands and settled the empty highlands of the interiors of Guyana, Jamaica, Trinidad and Dominica. On small, densely-populated islands such as Barbados, Antigua and St. Kitts the lack of such free land obliged former slaves to remain on the plantations as wage workers. Even elsewhere, the marginality of land available for peasant farming, plus the need to pay taxes, forced many to seek seasonal work on plantations, thus creating temporary migration currents and further social dislocation (Patterson, 1978).

Internal migration by black former slaves away from the plantations was viewed by the white plantocracy as a vicious symbolic action, and they retaliated by turning to other external sources of labour. The ex-slaves, in their turn, reacted against the arrival of Asian coolie migration with equal vehemence. This led to a mass exodus of large sections of the Afro-Caribbean population to surrounding regions – to Panama, where they constituted the bulk of the labour force which dug the Canal; to Nicaragua and Costa Rica, where the United Fruit Company was expanding its activities strongly and offered possibilities for agricultural wage labour; and later, in the 1920s, to the United States, where Jamaicans grouped in New York and Barbadians at Boston.

For the colonial plantation-owners, however, the real significance of the abolition of slavery was that labour became scarce and potentially expensive. The problem was solved by the coolie system, which had already been developing in the decade or so before slavery's abolition. 'Now', wrote Lydia Potts (1990, p. 62), exhibiting her Marxist credentials, 'it was the turn of the Asian peoples to become victims of exploitation and to be traded on the world market for labour power'. After the wiping out of the native Americans and Caribs and the wholesale plucking of slaves from Africa, 'the population of yet another continent was to be transformed into a reservoir of labour power and shunted around the world'.

The literature often uses the terms coolie and indentured labourer interchangeably, as I do. In fact, some distinction can be drawn. 'Indenture' refers to a clearly defined contractual relationship whereby the migrant labourer signed a contract in his or her country of origin which fixed the duration and terms of employment. It was not possible for the worker to terminate the contract before expiry – usually one or five but sometimes up to ten years. 'Coolieism' is a more collective term referring to indenture and other forms of highly constrained labour recruitment and migration which operated in the 19th and early 20th centuries.

In many respects indenture differed from slavery only in name. Workers were selected, processed and transported in much the same ways as the slaves who preceded them; they arrived at the same depots in the Caribbean, for instance; and they were often accommodated in the same barracks as were formerly occupied by the slaves. Rates of mortality, both at sea and at work, also replicated those of the slaves, especially during the early indenture period in the mid-19th century. Many workers died before their contracts were finished, the 'wages' were often cancelled out by fines and the purchase of the necessities of life, and forced renewal of contracts was widespread. Some contracts allowed for a free return passage, others did not. As with slavery there was a considerable gap between the regulations as enacted and as practised. Abuse of women was widespread. It was anything but free wage labour migration (Tinker, 1984).

The procurement of indentured labourers and coolies enabled former slave-owners to stock up with new supplies of cheap labour. The availability of coolies created wage competition with the former slaves and thus held down labour costs. Coolieism enabled the utilization of the vast labour reserves of more recently acquired colonies in Asia, as well as releasing that labour for use in colonial societies such as Australia which had not previously 'enjoyed' African slave labour.

The geography of coolie migration is much more complex than that of the transatlantic slave migrations, and the data sources are fragmented. The many different countries and regions affected recorded movements in different ways. The privateers responsible for managing the recruitment and transport of coolies often kept no records, or such records as existed were soon lost. Many migrations were seasonal, further complicating the statistics. There were two main source regions: India and China. The indications are that each suffered a net migration of 5–7 million coolies. For India, for instance, Davis (1951, p. 99) indicates an emigration of 30.2m. between 1834 and 1937, and a return of 24.1m. The vast majority of the movements represent indentured labourers but Davis's figures include some family members, some free workers during the 1920s and 1930s, and a certain quantity of traders and business migrants; they do not include the large-scale labour migrations which took place within British India such as those to the tea plantations of Assam. Indians' willingness to sign up for indenture was greatly increased by recurrent famines. People suffering from starvation were often picked up by recruitment agents, given food and persuaded to sign contracts with their thumbprints (Tinker, 1984, p. 119).

The second half of the 19th century saw the two main sources joined by three others: Java, Japan and some Melanesian and Micronesian islands. Even more various were the countries of arrival. Coolies were despatched not only to British colonies in various parts of the world (the Caribbean, Canada, East and South Africa, Australia, New Zealand, Fiji, Mauritius, Malaya etc.) but also to colonial territories owned by France, Germany, Holland, Belgium, Denmark, Spain and Portugal, as well as to the USA and some other countries. Table 1.2 lists more than 40 different countries which imported coolie labour, and this list is probably not a complete one. The complexity of the migration patterns increases when one realizes that some countries drew coolies from more than one source area, and that there was a considerable amount of coolie migration between recipient countries.

Indentured and other coolie labour was used to cultivate plantation crops (sugar, tea, coffee, rubber, tobacco, cotton); to mine gold, diamonds and tin; to dive for pearls; to construct roads, railways and canals; and to work in domestic service. In the Caribbean the previous correlation between sugar and slavery was replaced by that between

Table 1.2: The geography of coolie migration: the host countries

British colonies	German colonies
British Guyana (Demerara)	Samoa
Trinidad and Tobago	Nauru
Grenada	New Guinea
St. Lucia	
St. Vincent	**Dutch colonies**
Jamaica	Dutch Guiana (Surinam)
Antigua	Dutch East Indies
St. Kitts and Nevis	(Sumatra, Banka, Bilitung)
Canada (British Colombia)	
Uganda	**Danish colonies**
Natal	St Croix
Transvaal	
Cape Province	**Spanish colonies**
Mauritius	Cuba
Australia (Queensland)	
New Zealand	**Portuguese colonies**
Fiji	Mozambique
British North Borneo	
Ceylon	**Belgian colonies**
Burma	Congo
Assam	
British Malaya	**Other countries**
	USA (California)
French colonies	Hawaii
Réunion	Panama
Martinique	Peru
Guadeloupe	Thailand
French Guiana (Cayenne)	
Madagascar	
Society Islands	
New Caledonia	
Indochina	
French Polynesia	

Source: Potts, 1990, p. 67.

sugar and indentured labour, a process which has produced great plurality, and division, within Caribbean societies (Lowenthal, 1972). An early attempt to substitute slaves by Portuguese plantation workers from Madeira failed; the Portuguese, especially in Guyana, quickly switched to small-scale trading, an area that they continue to dominate today. Attempts in the 1850s and 1860s to introduce Chinese labour into Caribbean plantations also had unintended outcomes.

Many of the early arrivals died out or returned. Later ones survived by a curious set of expedients. The male coolies took black peasant concubines and the Afro-Chinese offspring were then shipped back to China where they were enculturated into Chinese ways by relatives, returning to the Caribbean as young adults with Chinese wives. Like the Portuguese before them, however, they seized the opportunities for entrepreneurship available in the post-emancipation economy and came to dominate small-scale retailing in Jamaica, Trinidad and elsewhere. More important demographically and more successful from the point of view of the plantation economy was the migration of Indian indentured migrants into Guyana, Trinidad and Jamaica. Today Indians comprise more than half the population of Guyana, 40 per cent of that of Trinidad and nearly 5 per cent of that of Jamaica (Ehrlich, 1971).

Outside of the Caribbean, waves of Indian indentured labourers have contributed greatly to the ethnic and cultural plurality of many other countries – East Africa (where Indian labour was used to build the Ugandan railway), Madagascar, Mauritius, Réunion, Fiji, Borneo, Malaya, Burma and Ceylon. As well as the strong association with sugar, they worked on rubber and tea plantations, in mines, rice mills and ports. Although India was a British colony, it allowed other colonial powers to avail themselves of the indenture system: hence the Dutch took Indians to Surinam, the French took Indians to Réunion and the Portuguese took some to Mozambique, for instance. Large-scale Indian coolie migrations also took place within the South Asian region – to Ceylon, Burma and Assam to work in tea plantations as well as for construction projects like the Burmese railways. These more local migrations, and those to Malaya, were mainly where alternatives to classic indenture were practised – for instance, the *Kangany* system where local plantation foremen (who were Indians) had the responsibility not only of supervising field labour but also of going to India to recruit new workers (Kondapi, 1951). Figure 1.4 is an attempt to map Indian coolie migrations of the late 19th and early 20th centuries to their main destinations as a way of summing-up some of the previous discussion.

Like India, China too was regarded by the European colonial powers as an inexhaustible supply of cheap labour. However, long before Europeans began to tap this source, Chinese workers were being exported to various parts of South-East Asia in a system controlled by Chinese business interests. For instance, Chinese businessmen ran the gold industry in Borneo and shipped over 30,000 coolies to work in the mines. Other Chinese-sponsored coolie migrations took place to Malaya, Indonesia and the Philippines. European colonial interests interlocked quickly with this Chinese migration infrastructure, and Chinese middlemen acted as recruiting and shipping agents.

Most of the coolies came from southern China and were moved out via Macao, Hong Kong and Shanghai. The last of these places gave its name to a particularly brutal form of capture of Chinese peasants who had come to the town to sell vegetables and other goods; such press-ganging of unsuspecting Chinese into work as coolies in unknown foreign destinations was widespread in China (Potts, 1990, pp. 85, 88).

The European powers not only recruited Chinese coolies to work in South-East Asia, their traditional labour market region, but also transported them further afield – to South Africa, Queensland, New Zealand, Western Samoa, Canada, California, the Caribbean (especially Cuba, Trinidad, Guyana and Surinam) and Peru. To take one specific example, in the early 1850s, 50,000 Chinese were imported to work the Californian gold mines and construct railways across the southern United States. This and some subsequent Chinese migrations to North America were managed by powerful Chinese syndicates operating a credit-ticket system. The syndicates, which operated from bases both in China and America (especially San Francisco), advanced passage money to the coolies and also controlled access to jobs and manipulated wage levels (Barth, 1964). The Chinese migration syndicates were an early example of migration being stage-managed by institutions from the sending country; up to that time nearly all labour migrations had been controlled by the colonial power at the receiving end.

The story of coolie migration is completed later in the 19th century and early in the 20th century when Oceania, Java and Japan supplied workers to various parts of the colonial and global labour markets. According to Graves (1984) the recruitment of 64,000 Pacific Islanders to work in the Queensland sugar estates between 1863 and 1906 was the most significant of the many migrations which took an estimated

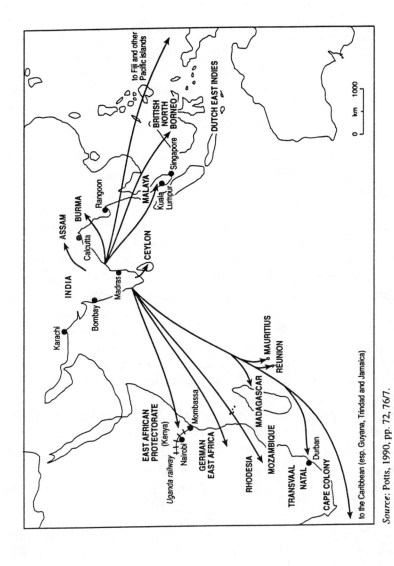

Source: Potts, 1990, pp. 72, 76/7.

Figure 1.4   Indian coolie migrations of the late 19th and early 20th centuries

29

280,000 Melanesians and Micronesians into indentured labour in Australia, Fiji, Samoa, Hawaii, New Caledonia, Nauru and Peru between 1840 and 1915. Like many indentured labourers, they were recruited by a mixture of kidnap, trickery and deals with local chiefs and middlemen. Males under thirty predominated, the contracts were for three years, and nearly all returned. What is especially interesting in Graves's account is his demonstration of how indenture was the end-product of a long historical process by which traders, missionaries, settlers and other colonial forces had disrupted the pre-capitalist communal fishing and farming economy, making the inhabitants increasingly dependent upon colonially-chosen products such as whaling and sandalwood. Once dislodged in this way, they became available for recruitment into the wider regional labour market.

Coolie migration in Dutch East India did not get under way as a mass phenomenon until the Dutch abandoned the 'culture system', by which peasants were forced to cultivate land under state directive, in 1871 (slavery having been already outlawed in 1860). The Coolie Ordinance came into force in 1880 in order to promote and regulate the supply of labour in a different way; it gave plantation-owners extensive rights over their newly-recruited coolie workers, who were treated as little more than slaves. Initial coolie migrations were from Madura to Java and from China to Sumatra. After 1911 there was a much more massive migration of Javanese to Sumatra; according to Kloosterboer (1960, p. 33) almost four-fifths of the 500,000 coolies employed in the Dutch colonies in 1911 were Javanese.

Finally, Japanese coolies migrated mainly to Hawaii and the USA: to the former as sugar workers, to the latter as farm labourers, domestic servants and as railway-builders (taking over in part from the Chinese in this activity). By 1910 there were 70,000 Japanese sugar workers in Hawaii and 100,000 Japanese living in the United States (Potts, 1990, pp. 96–7).

According to Potts (1990, pp. 71,73) the indenture system and its allied forms of coolie migration involved perhaps 37 million workers between 1834 and its final abolition in the Dutch East Indies in 1941. It thus eclipsed in magnitude, if not in its permanent effects, the slave migration that preceded it. Most of the indentured workers were young men, but as with slave migrations, some women and children also went. Shipments of indentured workers from India were supposed to contain 40 women per 100 men, but this was frequently not attained (Tinker, 1984, p. 79). Nevertheless the proportion of females was much higher amongst Indian coolies than amongst the Chinese. For this reason the Indians tended to remain abroad and evolve into settled communities, often facilitated by their transfer into peasant farming (e.g. rice farming in Guyana) or into trade and office work (e.g. in East Africa). The Chinese had higher rates of return, although several expatriate communities became firmly established, both within South-East Asia and elsewhere.

Like slavery, the coolie system was abolished piecemeal (Potts, 1990, pp. 97–100). Indentured labour – its harshest form – was abolished in 1878 in Malaya, in 1911 in Natal and Trinidad, in 1915 in Mauritius, in 1917 in British Guyana and in 1920 in Fiji and India. Abolition was gradual in another sense too, for the banning of indenture often merely led to only slightly milder forms of repressive labour recruitment; thus the *Kangany* system reached its peak after the outlawing of indentured labour. As mentioned above, the coolie system survived longest in the Dutch colonies, where the Coolie Ordinance was finally revoked in 1941.

Finally, it is important to appreciate the longer-term economic, political, ethnic and cultural legacies of the colonial migrations. Shifting and shunting people around the world in order to exploit their labour is morally utterly reprehensible. Such migrations have made their contribution to the creation and perpetuation of uneven development on a world scale. Another result has been the formation of multi-ethnic societies which cannot be 'unscrambled'. In some places a certain degree of fusion has come about through intermarriage and cross-breeding amongst the various racial groups – this is the case in Brazil and Cuba for instance. In other parts of the Caribbean the racial division between descendants of African slaves and Indian indentured labourers remains almost complete. Indeed several post-colonial inter-ethnic conflicts have their origins in the divisions brought about by indenture; the expulsion of Indians from East Africa and the more recent conflict in Fiji are cases in point. And today the roots of racist stereotyping in Europe and elsewhere often derive from the historical treatment of slaves and other colonized peoples.

ACROSS THE OCEANS: INTERNATIONAL MIGRATION UNTIL THE 1920'S

From the previous section we saw that indenture survived well into the 20th century. For our next historical 'type' of migration we have to overlap back in time to the early–mid-19th century when international migration started to change, both quantitatively and qualitatively, in quite dramatic terms. This was a time when Europeans came to dominate international and especially intercontinental migration and they moved on a scale previously unknown. Between 1850 and 1914 approximately 50 million Europeans emigrated intercontinentally: about 70 per cent of them to North America, 12 per cent to South America and 9 per cent to South Africa, Australia and New Zealand. Most of the remainder were intercontinental but overland migrants who left European Russia for Asiatic Siberia, together with a smaller quantity of French (about 1 million) who settled in North Africa. Looking at the figures by sending country, of the 50 million or so emigrants, 11 million were from Britain, 10 million from Italy, 7 million from Ireland, 6 million from Spain and Portugal, 5 million from Austria-Hungary, 5 million from Germany and 3 million from Scandinavian countries (Baines, 1991, pp. 7–9). Figure 1.5 shows the geographical pattern of this great European long-distance migration.

These figures, like most migration statistics, are rough-and-ready, but this does not detract from the fact that this was the maximum period of voluntary international migration in history (I shall comment on the true nature of this voluntariness shortly). Two other statistical points should be made. First, the figures are for one-way emigration out of Europe. They take no account of return moves. Data on return migration are generally much more shaky than the figures for emigration. What is certain is that rates of return varied both over time and from one country to another: generally they were higher than commonly realized. Second, the numbers mentioned in the previous paragraph refer only to actual migrants. Counting the descendants of those migrants would present us with a totally different picture.

It is common to present the 'great migration' of Europeans across the Atlantic as a voluntary migration composed of free-willed individuals (cf. Scott, 1968, p. 11; Beijer, 1969, p. 14). Whilst it is true that there were clear differences between the European settler

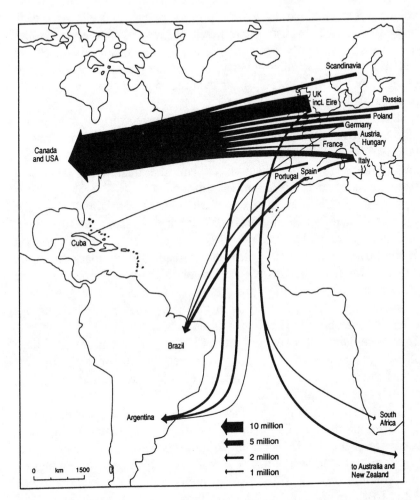

Source: Based on data in Baines, 1991; Segal, 1993, pp. 16, 17.

Figure 1.5   European long-distance migrations 1815-1914

migrations and the migrations of slavery and indenture, the degree of voluntariness should be examined carefully. Souden's (1984) study of white indentured labour in the Caribbean and American eastern seaboard was cited earlier. Even those European migrants who made individual choices in response to perceived employment opportunities did so within a highly structured context. The constraints on choice and information included poverty, the sheer ignorance of conditions in the New World, and the propaganda fed to prospective migrants by passage-brokers.

Denoon (1984, p. 193) after having surveyed turn-of-the-century migration to six settler countries concluded that the distinction between voluntary and involuntary movement was far from clear-cut and that any reliance on voluntarism to explain the quantity, quality and fluctuations of such migration was unfounded.

Also up for debate is the issue of whether the transatlantic migrants were true settlement migrants. Whilst it is again true that land settlement remained a widely-held goal, a relatively small proportion of the 50 million became prairie homesteaders or outback livestock farmers. Most ended up as true labour migrants earning wages in industries and construction projects or carving out a living in some poor niche service activity in the urban economies of the burgeoning cities. As Newbury (1975) has stressed, whereas most of the imperial Tropics remained largely agricultural in the post-indenture era, most of the imperial 'Open Spaces' produced rapid urbanization and industrialization, and it was in these new industrial cities that most migrants found their futures.

The constraints on migrants' choices also reflected wider economic and demographic trends. Brinley Thomas (1972) noted the interdependence of the two sides of the 'Atlantic economy'. Both capital and labour migrated transatlantically according to the alternating swings of the economy on each side. This economic relationship was true not only of Britain and the United States but also held for Britain and the other settler countries – Canada, Argentina and Australia. In this way Thomas saw the long-distance circulation of labour via migration waves back and forth across the Atlantic as part and parcel of the process of capitalist development, although he did not quite put it in these terms. Closely connected with this spatial mobility of labour was the changing technology of travel and transport; in the 19th century the steamship and the railway overcame many of the physical and time barriers to movement for migrants and their paymasters.

Economic pressure from the European end had fundamental demographic causes. In the 300 years following 1650 the European population increased from 100 million to 560 million, a rate of increase significantly greater than that of the rest of the world. As the death rate in Europe declined and the birth rate failed to respond to keep population growth in check, emigration functioned as a safety-valve to skim off a significant proportion of the surplus. Some of this excess migrated to areas whose specific economic role was to produce food to feed the remaining European populations. The escape-hatch function also probably averted social discontent; hence migration was a policy with political advantages for the ruling class (Marks and Richardson, 1984, p. 15).

The safety-valve theory can be examined with reference to some specific countries (Table 1.3). For instance, in Norway, one of the countries to send the highest ratio of emigrants to population, the population had doubled between 1800 and 1865. In neighbouring Sweden, where 19th-century industrial and urban growth were more rapid, emigration still removed 1.1 million people between 1840 and 1914, equivalent to 25 per cent of the Swedish natural increase. In Norway over the same period the proportion was 40 per cent. The most conspicuous example in history of famine-induced migration is the great migration of more than 1 million people from Ireland during and after the famine of the 1840s, the bulk of whom emigrated permanently to the United States. Irish emigration continued at very high rates throughout the remainder of the 19th century (Table 1.3), virtually halving the population in the process. No other European country has been so fundamentally affected by emigration. By contrast, there was relatively little emigration from France, Belgium and the Netherlands, and it was only after the 1880s that southern European countries come into the picture. In Germany emigration faded as industrialization gathered pace. In Britain industrialization did not so much staunch emigration as change its character; emigrants came less from rural areas and more from urban districts where they constituted artisan and factory working classes fleeing poverty and squalor (Grigg, 1980).

*Table 1.3   European overseas emigration 1861–1910
(average annual rates per '000)*

	1861–70	1871–80	1881–90	1891–00	1901–10
England	2.8	4.0	5.6	3.6	5.5
Scotland	4.6	4.7	7.1	4.4	9.9
Ireland	14.6	6.6	14.2	8.9	7.0
Norway	5.8	4.7	9.5	4.5	8.3
Sweden	3.1	2.4	7.0	4.1	4.2
Finland	–	–	1.3	2.3	5.5
Denmark	–	2.1	3.9	2.2	2.8
Netherlands	0.6	0.5	1.2	0.5	0.5
Belgium	–	–	0.9	0.4	0.6
France	0.2	0.2	0.3	0.1	0.1
Germany	–	1.5	2.9	1.0	0.5
Switzerland	–	1.3	3.2	1.4	1.4
Austria-Hungary	–	0.3	1.1	1.6	4.8
Italy	–	1.1	3.4	5.0	10.8
Spain	–	–	3.6	4.4	5.7
Portugal	1.9	2.9	3.8	5.1	5.7

Source: Baines, 1991, p. 10.

Students of transatlantic migration writing from the American end offered both complementary and different perspectives to those from Europe. For them the movement carried with it the resonance of the words enshrined on the pedestal of the Statue of Liberty: 'Give me your tired, your poor, your huddled masses yearning to be free'. America was the new land of opportunity, offering the dream of becoming an independent farmer or trader. This image of spaciousness and of boundless optimism was ruthlessly projected by emigration agencies and steamship companies which made fat profits from the 'human trade'. Often this dream led only to disillusionment – the migrants became rootless labourers building roads or railways, cowboys on large cattle ranches, or overworked factory hands. Yet a considerable proportion did live to see the realization of their dream, which was also the American dream, becoming prosperous farmers, white-collar workers or business people; while others were at least able to see their children achieve education and upward social mobility (Castles and Miller, 1993, p. 51).

It is also important to realize that, in spite of its mass nature, transatlantic migration was a selective process. The emigrants were never a random sample of the population from which they were drawn: differences of age, sex, income and other variables were often very marked. Moreover this differentiation varied from place to place and over time. In some regions it was the poorest who left; in others the poorest were too poor to afford the ticket for the voyage. Some, like the Irish famine migrants, left for good, intending never to return. Others migrated temporarily, returning home after a few years to build a new house or buy a plot of land in their village. Yet others intended to migrate temporarily, but ended up as permanent settlers, contributing to the ethnic hotch-potch out of which modern American society has been created.

Writing from the American perspective Piore (1979) distinguished between the 'old' immigration from North-West Europe which predominated over most of the 19th century, and the 'new' immigration from Eastern and Southern Europe which took over in the late 19th century and was brought to an end by World War I and the closing of unrestricted immigration by the United States in the early 1920s. The 'old' migration countries – Britain, Ireland, Germany, Scandinavia – sent migrants mainly in family groups for permanent settlement. Amongst the 'new' immigrants, who made up 78 per cent of the flow into the United States during the first decade of the 20th century, there was much temporary movement – single men, in particular, who worked in America for a couple of years and then returned home to their families. American scholars, committed to the ideal of the United States as a land of settled immigrants transforming themselves into American citizens, have generally overlooked the importance of return migration. The data are fragmentary, but they do show that whereas only about one in six of the 'old' immigrants returned, rates of return for Italians, Spaniards, Greeks, Croatians and Slovaks were 50–70 per cent (Baines, 1991, p. 39).

So much has been written by American scholars (and non-scholars!) on the 19th- and early 20th-century immigration to the United States that it is difficult to know where to even begin to summarize this vast literature. Much of it is parochial and characterized by filiopietism – the nostalgic contribution of this or that immigrant group to a particular town or district. Lacking true anthropological rigour, such studies are of little value in contributing to broad-brush treatments of the experience of immigrant workers in North America. Where broad, synthetic treatments have been attempted, they have often been based on dubious theoretical premises. Such a criticism has some relevance when applied, for example, to the important work of Robert Park and the 'Chicago School' of urban sociology in which the 'assimilation' of immigrants played the key role. Park's work in the 1920s and 1930s has been immensely influential (see Park (1950) for a collection of his significant writings) and generated a large following in different parts of the world and across various disciplines (Park and his Chicago colleague Burgess became very influential in urban geography for instance), but his physiological analogies of 'competition', 'conflict', 'assimilation' etc. which derived from his Social Darwinian background, and his assumption that all immigrants would eventually conform to some kind of Anglo-Saxon American 'norm', were highly questionable bases for the undoubtedly impressive empirical studies of the Chicago School (cf. Price, 1969, pp. 213–17). French-Canadians, to name but one group, were not impressed by such a stance!

What I shall try to do by way of summarizing the character and impact of European immigration to North America is to make three main points – about the economic impact of this immigration, about its human character, and about the role of chain migration and social networks.

First, immigrant labour has played a vitally important role in the United States economy, although the precise nature and scale of its impact are impossible to measure. Slavery had been a major source of labour, and hence capital accumulation, in the country's early history when plantation crops were key products; these crops were strategic to the subsequent phase of industrial development which accelerated after the Civil War of 1861–65. However, the abolition of slavery and restrictions on the internal migration of black Americans (whose labour was still needed in the agricultural South) meant that new industry had largely to be staffed by mass immigration from Europe. Hence immigrants' patterns of settlement were linked to the emerging needs of the industrial economy. Just as influxes of Dutch, German and Scandinavian migrants developed links to particular agricultural areas of the Mid-West and Canada earlier in the 19th century, so labour recruited by canal and railway companies led to settlements of

Irish and Italians along these transport construction routes. Irish and Italians were also strongly attracted to east coast ports of arrival such as New York and Boston, where work was available in port industries, factories and construction sites. The development of heavy industry in Mid-West cities around the turn of the century attracted influxes of Central and Eastern European migrants – for instance Polish immigrants in the Pittsburg steel mills. In this way the American industrial working classes evolved along ethnic lines which often had marked geographical and occupational expression (Portes and Rumbaut, 1990).

Although most of the immigrants by the later 19th century were relatively unskilled and uneducated people from rural backgrounds in South and East Europe who were entering urban occupations and thereby providing relatively cheap labour for American industrial expansion, there was, throughout the American immigration experience, an important skilled component. This was responsible for technology transfer and the migration of particular industrial specialisms – Lancashire textile experts to New England, Staffordshire potters to Princeton, New Jersey, and Cornish hard rock miners to Wisconsin, Montana and California for example. In fact, throughout the 19th century many skilled industrial migrants, especially from Britain, were to be found in mining, metallurgy, engineering, textiles and other specialized industries in many parts of the world, often because the decline of an industry in Europe coincided with its growth elsewhere (Baines, 1991, p. 61).

Clearly, immigrants were not an undifferentiated mass of labour, a fact that American policy-makers came increasingly to confront after the 1880s. In economic policy terms, much of the 19th century following the mercantilism of the slave era until the 1880s could be regarded as a period of liberalism which was applied to trade, migration and transport infrastructure alike. European (and other) immigration to the United States was allowed to ebb and flow of its own accord, guided mainly by the fluctuating economic barometers of both Europe and America. The 1880s saw the era of unregulated immigration into the USA come to an end with the passing of exclusionary laws to keep out Chinese and other Asians; for Europeans and Latin Americans entry remained free until 1920. Restrictive immigration policies took various forms designed to exert greater control on the nationality, 'quality', and length of stay of immigrants. Some were founded on the positive or negative selection or rejection of immigrants with respect to some characteristic of perceived economic or political concern – for example the Literacy Acts of 1917 (USA) and 1919 (Canada). Other measures sought to control entry and length of stay by the need to perform some type of task or achieve some kind of target (Zolberg, 1978, p. 273).

Since the majority of immigrants were young adults at the peak of their productive potential, the American economy could be regarded as receiving a free gift of human capital carrying with them the costs of their upbringing. Hence the economy, in a growth scenario, could achieve greater output and capital investment. Neal and Uselding (1972) calculated that this enabled the USA to gain a minimum of five years' investment from immigration. Even bolder calculations were made by Spengler (1958) who estimated that, had no post-1840 immigration occurred, the USA population in 1940 would have been 85 million instead of 132 million. These calculations make some big assumptions, but they do point to the two-way relationship between migration and development in the receiving countries. At a simple level migrant labourers are not only producers but also consumers; their demand for goods and services has encouraged further growth of the American economy. More complexly, immigrants made it easier for productive expansion and technological change to occur and because technological development changed the character of the labour market, differentiating high- from low-skill jobs, it opened up new possibilities for unskilled immigrants to enter at the bottom of the industrial labour hierarchy (Baines, 1991, p. 62).

Secondly, these economic analyses of the effects of emigration on industrial development and the labour market should not be allowed to obscure the quite extraordinary personal hardships involved in transatlantic migration. The classic study by Thomas and Znaniecki (1918) on *The Polish Peasant in Europe and America* was one of the first to demonstrate the contrasting worlds of the emigrant – peasant Europe and urban America; the loss of one and the gradual coming to terms with the other. A later study by Oscar Handlin (1951), appropriately entitled *The Uprooted*, tried to explore the meaning of separation from the Old World. Amongst many evocative passages, Handlin wrote:

The peasants had been cut off from homes and villages, homes and villages which were not simply places, but communities in which was deeply enmeshed a whole pattern of life. They had left familiar fields and hills, the cemetery in which their fathers rested, the church, the people, the animals, the trees they had known in the intimate context of their being.

Handlin went on to describe the awful urban conditions in which these rural Europeans had to settle – in the cramped North End of Boston; in murky East Side New York, hemmed in against the river; or in Chicago over and against the slaughterhouses. Migrants who had lived most of their lives out of doors in tune with nature and the seasons suddenly had as their homes airless, sunless garrets with extreme lack of space, privacy and facilities. Of course, this is not to ignore the conditions which made them emigrants in the first place – lack of land, oppressive landlords, poverty, hunger, hopelessness. But not a few were bitterly disappointed that they had made the trip.

Handlin's work has been criticized for overemphasizing the chasm between the migrants' origin and destination and for arguing that immigrants had to make a clean break from their European past in order to succeed in the United States (cf. Baines, 1991, p. 79). Recent studies, particularly those which focus on Italian transatlantic migration, have overcome this limitation by identifying the key role played by kinship and social networks in the migration process. This is my third theme on European transatlantic migration and it also enables us to highlight the importance of the process of chain migration.

Chain migration has undoubtedly been a key mechanism by which long-distance migration out of Europe was reproduced over time. The often-quoted paper by MacDonald and MacDonald (1964) lays great emphasis on the role of primary kinship ties in the operation of chain migration but the relationship can be widened to include all friendship and contact patterns that existed in the tightly-knit rural communities of Europe in the 19th century. Chain migration functioned to overcome many of the uncertainties about transatlantic emigration. Contacts from the same village, especially if they were relatives, could thus be relied upon to ease the transition so that the new emigrant could pass 'from known to known' and perhaps get help towards finding a job and somewhere to live. Employees often asked existing immigrant employees to suggest new recruits to the enterprise if it was hiring extra labour.

Chain migration also led to very specific geographical patterning of migration processes. It explained, to a certain extent, inter-village and inter-provincial contrasts in rates and destinations of emigration, and it led to a situation in which the emigrants from one particular village or district would be found concentrated in one or a small number of destinations. Moreover, within the destination setting, chain migration and community cohesion often led to the tight clustering of an emigrant group within a particular quarter of a city (Bodnar, 1985). The cases of the 'little Italies' of Chicago and other American cities became particularly famous.

Chain migration to North America affected northern and southern Europeans alike; it probably was less important for British and Irish emigrants who were going to a place where their own language and culture were dominant. The literature on European transatlantic migration is full of examples of chain migration; just a couple of cases can be mentioned here. According to Hvidt (1975), chain migration was the predominant pattern amongst the 300,000 Danes who emigrated to North America between 1840 and 1914. Towards the end of the 19th century a quarter of all Danish migrants to the USA went on steamship tickets prepaid by Danish emigrants already in America. Although for Denmark as a whole there was a general inverse correlation between a district's income and its rate of outmigration, much of the localized effect of emigration could be explained by chain migration. For Italy, several brief examples are given in an appendix to the paper by MacDonald and MacDonald (1964), whilst many more detailed cases can be found in the abundant literature on Italian–American migration. Sometimes family and community-based chain migration was combined with 'occupational chaining' whereby migrants from the same origin would also do the same job in the destination setting. Again Italian examples are prolific: fruit-sellers from Termini Imerese in Sicily, bootblacks from Viggiano in Basilicata, street musicians from the hill villages of northern Tuscany, ice-cream sellers from the Val Cadore in the Venetian Alps (King, 1992).

Potential emigrants obtained information about emigration possibilities from their relatives and friends in two main ways: from letters, and from emigrants returning home. Returnees became notorious for exaggerating the success of their own migration project: ostentatious behaviour and lavish displays of wealth acted as a strong incentive for others to make the move (see Gilkey, 1967). Letters were obviously a more private and personal inducement to migration. However, even these could become public property: in Ireland, where there was a great deal of illiteracy, letters would be read aloud by the village priest (Schrier, 1959, p. 41).

Before we leave the fortune-seeking long-distance migrations of the 19th and early 20th centuries, I want to mention briefly some other examples which were happening at roughly the same time, for they are important in helping us to understand how different economic systems and cultures have evolved in various parts of the world. The North Atlantic migrations which I have concentrated on in this section were paralleled by other large flows, mainly of permanent settlers, from southern Europe to South America. Italy sent 2.4 million migrants to Argentina and 1.4 million to Brazil. Portugal also sent 1.4 million to Brazil, to join those who had already settled this part of South America in the previous centuries; Spain likewise sent 2–3 million to the remainder of Latin America. Britain and Ireland continued to send settler-migrants to South Africa, Australia and New Zealand. Some of those sent to Australia were 'convict-migrants' – another form of involuntary migration. The Australian example allows me to re-stress the point that the interrelationship between intercontinental migration and global economic forces is not new. The Australian colonies functioned within the British Empire as suppliers of raw materials such as wool, wheat and gold; the production of these goods could only be expanded through a supply of labour from outside. When the supply from the British Isles was no longer sufficient, Britain encouraged Australia, as we have seen, to import labour from elsewhere in the Empire – from India, China and the South Pacific Islands (Castles and Miller, 1993, p. 53).

Alongside these major migrations were many others of less numerical importance but intriguing because of their contribution to the ethnic diversity and character of the destination setting. For instance, considerable numbers of Japanese settled in Peru (up to 1907) and Brazil (after 1908); President Fujimora of Peru is of Japanese ancestry. Another fascinating example of a historical migration flow lending a particular character to a place is the Welsh migration to Patagonia, Argentina, during 1865–88. This was an attempt to conserve Welsh emigrants' culture by settling them in an area remote from British (i.e. English) colonial influence. Today 20,000 people in Patagonia are of Welsh descent including 5,000 who are bilingual Welsh/Spanish (Bowen, 1966). Clearly, the world would be a much less interesting place without international migration!

EUROPE WITHIN AND BEYOND: *GASTARBEITER* MIGRATION

I now move on to examine the characteristics of modern migrations, mainly those since the end of World War II. Once again, we shall identify many types of migration, some of which have their historical parallels in the migratory phenomena already described, and others of which will be new to our analysis. Within Europe we shall concentrate on the so-called 'guestworker' migrations of the 1950s, 1960s and early 1970s. We shall then more briefly note three other important target areas for international migration – North America, Australia and the Persian Gulf – and compare the characteristics of their labour migrations and policies with those of Europe.

The postwar era witnessed the changing nature of global relations from their colonial and imperial expressions to the spread of economic empires based on the hegemony of capital. This statement needs to be qualified in two ways. First, as my earlier account showed, colonialism was at base an early form of international capitalism, structured through imperial conquest and international control. Second, with regard to labour migration, postwar international flows contain within them powerful echoes of the earlier colonial periods: for instance the migration to Britain of hundreds of thousands of Irish, West Indians, Indians and Pakistanis. However, the lack of a significant colonial empire did not prevent other countries from encouraging the mass immigration of labour when it was beneficial for them to do so – as the cases of Germany and Switzerland illustrate.

I shall come back to the case of West Germany very soon, for it is the best example of how labour migration was used as an explicit instrument of policy to promote economic growth. Before I do so, let us throw a backward glance. Earlier, we saw how Europe was a continent of massive net emigration overseas. At the same time, however, and even before, there were also important labour migrations going on within Europe. These took place largely from areas of rural poverty and overpopulation towards growing commercial and industrial districts, coalfields and towns in other regions and other countries. Lucassen (1987) has carried out a detailed survey of these intra-European movements of migrant labour at the dawn of the industrial era, drawing particular inspiration from a questionnaire administered by the French Empire during 1808–13. There was a large-scale drift to the economically active North Sea coast where seasonal labourers from as far away as Germany and Poland found work cutting grass on dairy farms, harvesting wheat and digging peat. Other migrants worked in construction and hydraulic projects, brick works and small-scale industries. Using the French data and other sources Lucassen mapped areas of labour inflow and outflow for the whole of Europe. The major migrant-attracting areas were the North Sea coastlands from Calais to the Danish border, eastern England, the Paris Basin, the French Midi, Castile in central Spain and north-central Italy. Lucassen concluded (1987, p. 215) that these systems of temporary migrant labour served not merely a transitional function but 'constituted a basic and integral part of the economic and social development of Europe'.

Larger-scale and more permanent migrations of labour came with the Industrial Revolution in Europe. In 1845 Engels wrote that 'the rapid expansion of English industry could not have taken place if England had not had in the large and poor population of Ireland a reserve army of labour of which to avail itself'. Already by 1851 there were 727,000 Irish immigrants in Britain, representing 3 per cent of the population of England and over 7 per cent of the population of Scotland. Particular concentrations were to be found in Liverpool and Glasgow: the 'Irish' character of these cities persists to this day. Engels went on to describe the appalling living and working conditions of the Irish in industrial Britain in the mid-19th century (Engels, 1962). But there were also other forms of Irish migration to Britain: groups of potato-harvesters, some as young as eleven or twelve, travelled every summer from Donegal and Mayo to the farms of lowland Scotland; and mobile gangs of Irish labourers came to dig the canals (or navigations – hence the term 'navvies') and lay the railways of Britain. The Irish link with the construction industry persists; the potato-picking migration died out in the 1960s (Jackson, 1963).

France, too, attracted large quantities of immigrants in the 19th century, especially between 1851 and 1881, by which date there were 1 million foreigners present, 2.7 per cent of the French population. Italians were the largest group, numbering 300,000 by the end of the century (plus another 300,000 who had taken French nationality). The foreign workers carried out unskilled manual labour in agriculture, mines and factories – the heavy, dirty jobs that French workers were less willing to undertake. Foreign labour also played a significant role in German industrialization. The base industries and mines of the Ruhr attracted Polish labour from the overcrowded agricultural estates of East Prussia: by 1913, 40 per cent of the Ruhr's 400,000 coal miners were Polish. In 1907 there were 800,000 foreign workers in Germany, making up over 4 per cent of the labour force. Half of them worked in industry, a third in agriculture and one-tenth in trade and transport.

In contrast to France where family migration has often been permitted and French citizenship relatively readily offered, migrant workers in Germany were subject to strict control regimes which enabled the authorities to prevent them from remaining in Germany during non-productive periods – a policy which was to re-emerge in the 1960s, as we shall see. At the beginning of the 20th century Polish agricultural workers were forced to leave Germany every winter: this not only facilitated the optimum exploitation of Polish labour, it also prevented them from becoming resident and diluting the 'purity' of the German population. At the same time compulsory 'legitimation' tied industrial migrants to a particular urban place of work where their over-exploitation often led to the destruction of their health. Exploitation of foreign labour power by Germany reached its most brutal forms during the two world war periods. Concentration camp detainees (mainly Jews and gypsies), prisoners of war and deportees from Poland, the Soviet Union and France were the main source of labour power for the Nazis' 'extermination through work' policies. Towards the end of World War II foreign civilian workers and prisoners of war numbered 7–8 million and constituted about a quarter of the German Reich's labour force (Potts, 1990, pp. 137–41).

The early postwar years saw the rapid development of labour

migration focused on the stronger economies of Western Europe – France, Britain, Switzerland, the Benelux countries and, a little later, West Germany. During the 1950s and 1960s the various migration flows evolved into a complex international system transferring millions of workers from the mainly rural peripheral regions of Europe to the industrial and urban regions of the 'core'. The sending countries were of two types: colonial and ex-colonial countries such as India, Pakistan and the British, French and Dutch Caribbean territories; and countries on the margins of Europe – Ireland, Finland, and the Mediterranean countries. Intra-EEC labour migration (largely from Italy to France, West Germany and Belgium) was facilitated by Community legislation for the free movement of workers, but more important were the many bilateral agreements drawn up between the European countries of labour demand and a wide range of labour supply countries stretching from Portugal to Turkey across southern Europe and down to West African countries like Senegal, Togo and Mauritania (Salt and Clout (eds), 1976). By the early 1970s about 10 million migrant workers were living in Europe: a massive stateless group of people equivalent to the population of a medium-sized European country like Belgium or Portugal.

Figure 1.6 is an attempt to map these pre-1973 flows and Table 1.4 presents some simple time-series data for a selection of immigrant countries.

Economic equilibrium arguments in favour of labour migration were deployed and became attractive, in different ways, to the governments of both sending and receiving countries. The former saw themselves as getting some relief from unemployment and the resulting social and political pressures. The latter saw labour immigration as an aspect of economic growth allowing both a faster expansion of production and an anti-inflationary source of preserving low wages (Kindleberger, 1967). Empirically it was in fact true that the countries experiencing high net immigration during 1945–73 – West Germany, Switzerland, France (and Australia) – tended to have higher economic growth rates than those, like the UK and USA at that time, which had lower net immigration.

Let us now return to examine the case of West Germany as the archetype. After the erection of the Berlin Wall in 1961 cut off the supply of labour from Poland and East Germany, the rapidly-growing

West German economy sought labour elsewhere. Initially it found ready supplies in Italy, fellow member of the fledgling Common Market. However, this period coincided with the rapid growth of the Italian economy, and the south Italian peasants who might have migrated to German industrial jobs (or followed their ancestors overseas) found 'intervening opportunities' in factory jobs in northern Italian cities like Milan and Turin (King, 1976). German capital had to search elsewhere for cheap labour, and during the 1960s bilateral recruitment agreements were signed with Greece, Spain, Portugal, Yugoslavia, Turkey and Morocco. The postwar chronology of labour migration into West Germany illustrates this widening search for workers to drive the growth of German industry and perform the low-status service jobs (sweeping streets, cleaning offices etc.) that the German workers refused to do.

Table 1.5 illustrates Germany's enlarging international hinterland for migrant workers in Mediterranean Europe: initially Italians were the largest group in the stock of foreign workers, then Yugoslavs and Turks.

The West German policy has been to use foreign labour as fuel for the engine of economic growth, but also as a cushion against unemployment for the German workforce. The German strategy of *Konjunkturpuffer* was quite explicit: migrant labour was to be used as a *buffer* against *conjunctures* or economic cycles. To this day Germany officially denies that it is a country of immigration: the foreign workers are *Gastarbeiter* or temporarily residing guest-workers.

Guestworker migration into West Germany occurred in its 'purest' form during the 1960s. Foreign workers were hired direct from their home countries by German recruitment offices set up all over the Mediterranean regions of supply. Many writers drew parallels with the past and called the *Gastarbeiter* the slaves of modern Europe; Robin Cohen (1987) for example called them the 'new helots', after the inhabitants of Helos who were enslaved by the Spartans of Ancient Greece. The recruitment centres had medical units to ensure that only healthy young adults were admitted. Those passed fit were marked with a felt-tip pen, an act which recalled the branding of African slaves noted earlier. A long train journey – three days from Turkey – then transported them to start their 'other' life, where they were

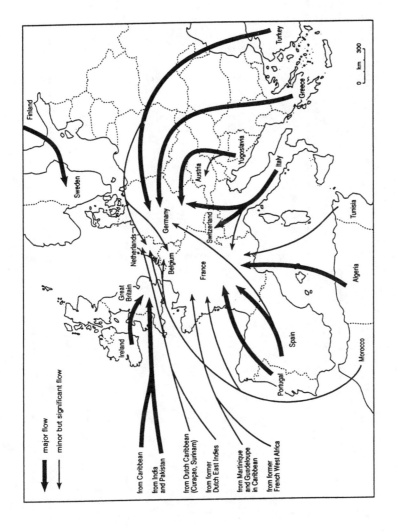

Figure 1.6   Labour migration into European industrial countries, 1945/73

49

Table 1.4 *Total and foreign populations in selected European countries, 1950s–1970s*

Year	Total (millions)	Foreign (thousands)	%	Year	Total (millions)	Total (thousands)	%
France				**West Germany**			
1954	43.2	1,766.1	4.1	1955	52.4	484.8	0.9
1960	45.9	1,633.4	3.6	1961	56.2	686.2	1.2
1965	49.0	2,683.5	5.5	1968	60.2	2,381.1	4.0
1970	50.0	3,393.5	6.6	1970	60.7	2,976.5	4.9
1974	53.6	4,128.3	7.7	1974	62.1	4,127.4	6.7
Belgium							
1954	8.8	379.5	4.3	1956	11.0	106.5	1.0
1961	9.2	453.5	4.9	1960	11.6	107.0	0.9
1965	9.5	636.7	6.7	1964	12.2	134.8	1.1
1970	9.7	696.3	7.2	1968	12.8	181.4	1.4
1973	9.8	775.2	7.9	1973	13.5	282.4	2.1
Switzerland							
1950	4.7	285.4	6.0	1954	7.2	111.1	1.5
1960	5.4	569.9	10.5	1960	7.5	190.6	2.5
1965	9.5	810.2	13.5	1968	7.9	320.6	4.0
1970	6.3	982.9	15.7	1970	8.1	411.3	5.1
1974	6.4	1,064.5	16.5	1974	8.2	401.2	4.9

Note: The percentage calculation are based on the full detailed figures.
Source: Hoffmann-Nowotny, 1978, pp. 90–91.

Table 1.5 Foreign guestworker population in West Germany, 1961–1974

Country of origin	Absolute numbers ('000)				0%			
	1961	1968	1971	1974	1961	1968	1971	1974
Italy	196.7	514.6	589.8	629.6	28.7	21.6	17.2	15.3
Spain	44.2	206.9	270.4	272.7	6.4	8.7	7.9	6.6
Portugal	–	37.5	75.2	121.5	–	1.6	2.2	2.9
Greece	42.1	271.3	394.9	406.4	6.1	11.4	11.5	9.9
Yugoslavia	16.4	331.6	594.3	707.8	2.4	13.9	17.3	17.2
Turkey	6.7	322.4	652.8	1027.8	1.0	13.5	19.0	24.9
Other	380.1	696.8	853.3	961.6	55.4	29.3	24.9	23.3
Total	686.2	2381.1	3430.7	4127.4	100.0	100.0	100.0	100.0

Source: Hoffmann-Nowotny, 1978, pp. 94–95.

housed in single-sex hostels close by their place of work. Both men and women were hired and accommodated in this way: the men for heavy industry and the women for light industry and cleaning jobs. By giving the migrants annual contracts which could be renewed or revoked at the whim of the employer, German capital was assured of a flexible labour supply which could be repatriated during a recession – as happened during 1966–67 when the number of migrant workers in West Germany dropped by a third. The constant 'rotation' of foreign workers minimized their ability to put down roots in West Germany. Thus the German economy was relieved of the costs of reproduction of labour – the feeding, clothing and upbringing of migrants had already been taken care of by their home countries. By admitting only single workers, social support costs for families were avoided. And by returning them to their home countries through the rotation policy, no costs of non-productive old age were incurred. Such was the theory and the practice of *Konjunkturpuffer* (Hoffmann-Nowotny, 1978).

During the 1970s, the *Konjunkturpuffer* strategy broke down. Partly stimulated by European Community legislation favouring the rights of immigrant workers, and partly driven by the realization that many migrants wanted to stay in Germany at all costs, a different attitude took hold and many migrants were allowed to bring in their families. Thus although worker migration tailed off after the 1973 oil crisis (the stock of migrant workers in Germany dropped from 2.6 million in 1973 to 1.5 million by the mid-1980s), the migration of family members increased, as did the total stock of foreign population, which reached 5.2 million in 1990.

Lydia Potts gives a more cynical interpretation of this policy shift. According to her, the policy of reuniting families shifted responsibility for the reproduction of labour power from the hostel to the family and was aimed at the medium-term planning of the West German labour market. The children of the migrants, educated partly or wholly in Germany, and emerging from that education with few qualifications, represented an important source of labour for those sectors of the job market which required little in the way of formal academic achievement – the very sectors rejected by the more educationally privileged German youth. Moreover, unlike immigrants who enter a country as adults, the 'second generation' have the advantage of having learned to live with adaptive difficulties and language problems as children and at school (Potts, 1990, p. 144).

By far the most paradoxical aspect of the German migration experience is the fact that the government refuses to acknowledge that Germany is a country of immigration despite a presence of over 5 million foreigners, many of whom have been in the country now for 20 years or more. Time and again government documents and officials repeat the mantra: 'The Federal Republic is not an immigration country. Germany is a place of residence for foreigners who will eventually return home voluntarily.' The reasons for this strange stance derive from the philosophy of German society whereby nation, people and place (or territory) are organized in a very particular way. Briefly, *Volk* (the German people) takes precedence over *Reich* (the state). The highly exclusionary model of German citizenship is based on *ius sanguini*, the 'law of blood'. In the past this was used to take citizenship (and life) away from Jews and gypsies because they allegedly lacked German blood. By the same token Turks who have been in Germany for perhaps 30 years, including children born in Germany who may never have set foot in Turkey, are denied the chance of becoming citizens, or even of being acknowledged as settled immigrants. Naturalization is extremely hard to obtain. Foreign workers remain disconnected legally and emotionally with the place where they live and work, and their children are not fully part of the society into which they were born. Even second-generation immigrants live in a state of insecurity and can, under some circumstances – conviction for a criminal offence or long-term unemployment – be deported to the country of origin of their parents (Castles and Miller, 1993, p. 115).

The German situation is in stark contrast to that in some other countries, such as Australia and France, where the inclusionary model of *ius soli* ('law of the soil') operates and grants citizenship to anyone born in the country as well as to those who have been resident there for a certain number of years. The German paradox has become even more bizarre since 1989 with the welcoming and granting of automatic citizenship to 'ethnic Germans' from countries like Romania and Bulgaria. In many cases the origin of the German connection may be several generations back in time, and the *Volk* may speak no German!

European labour migration such as that from Turkey to Germany, or from Portugal to France, or Morocco to the Netherlands, can be linked to important debates on spatially uneven development. The interplay between migration and economic development in the areas sending and receiving migrants has been interpreted in a number of ways. Traditionally migration was seen as an equalizing mechanism, moving workers from labour surplus to labour deficit regions to the benefit of both. In this neoclassic equilibrium approach, individual migrants responded to the market by moving to areas where jobs were available and wages higher: this reduced the surplus of labour in their home areas so that wages there would rise to approach those in the richer destination areas. Supporters of the *Gastarbeiter* model pointed to a number of supposed advantages for the source regions: reduced unemployment, foreign exchange inflows in the form of remittances, and the return of the migrants themselves, richer and wiser, to their home countries.

The truth has turned out to be rather different. Quite apart from an unwillingness on the part of many migrants to return, those who do have usually only 'learnt' to sweep the streets, clean offices, or perform a simple manual task on a production line. Their health and mental well-being have often deteriorated, and their savings may turn out to be less than anticipated because of high costs of living abroad.

Post-neoclassical interpretations of international labour migration have for some time recognized that real people do not necessarily behave rationally; that there is a tendency for political, bureaucratic and monopolistic factors to constrain 'free market' behaviour; and that it is regional rates of growth rather than differences in absolute levels of income which best explain migration flows (Knox, 1984, p. 31). Now, many authors see migration as maintaining or even exaggerating economic and social disparities between countries and regions. In other words, as well as being a response to uneven development, migration is an expression of spatial inequality and further shapes and structures its future forms creating above all ties of dependency between sending and receiving countries. Castles and Kosack (1973) were amongst the first to regard labour migration as a form of development aid – the export of the finest and fittest – given by the poor to the rich countries. The relegation of migrant workers to the lowest rungs of the occupational ladder in the metropolitan country often 'deskills' workers who already had a certain level of education and training, perhaps as skilled farmers, artisans or mechanics. Investment in this education and training, and in the entire upbringing of the individual, thus represents a loss of 'human capital' from the point of view of the sending country. In its most extreme form this constitutes a 'brain drain', a term which was originally coined in the 1960s to portray the loss of British scientists to the United States, but which today refers to the loss of academics, doctors and students from Third World countries in favour of developed countries.

My concentration on Europe and in particular on the German case must now be tempered with some reference to other parts of the world. This will enable comparisons to be made with the German experience with *Gastarbeiter*, as well as providing further evidence to discuss the relationships between labour migration, capitalist development and international inequality.

First, it should be pointed out that not all European industrial countries have operated their mechanisms of immigration according to the *Gastarbeiter* model. Switzerland certainly has, carefully controlling its foreign labour supplies by means of a graduated system of permits involving no fewer than four categories: frontier, seasonal, annual and permanent migrants. In France, Belgium and the Netherlands some elements of the *Gastarbeiter* philosophy are observable, especially in the 1950s and early 1960s, but generally these countries have adopted more liberal policies of integration and settlement, although all followed Germany in halting worker immigration in the mid-1970s in response to economic crisis, socio-political pressures and rising unemployment. In the cases of Britain and Sweden permanent settlement was more or less encouraged right from the start, although attitudes have subsequently hardened.

In fact the United Kingdom experience of immigration stands apart from that of the rest of Europe on several counts. Here, migration from former colonies has been overwhelmingly dominant. Nineteenth-century immigration from Ireland, Britain's traditional labour reserve, was mentioned earlier. The Irish source bulked large again after the end of World War II: a net inflow of 350,000 between 1946 and 1960. Irish workers were particularly important as manual labour for industry and construction. Those engaged in construction projects, either buildings or major civil engineering works like motorways or airports, tended to be geographically mobile and widely dispersed.

Those who settled into factory jobs created distinct Irish communities in the industrial towns which were booming in the 1950s and 1960s – places like Birmingham, Coventry and Luton, centres of the rapidly-expanding car industry. Unlike immigrants in most continental European countries, Irish residents in Britain enjoy all civil rights including the right to vote.

Starting in the early 1950s, Commonwealth citizens started to arrive in Britain in significant numbers, first from the Caribbean and then from India and Pakistan. Some came as a result of direct recruitment – e.g. by London Transport in the Caribbean – but most came spontaneously in response to labour demand. By 1961 there were 540,000 people of New Commonwealth origin in Britain. Once the slack in the labour market had been taken up, however, there emerged a public and political reaction against black immigrants in which racial prejudice played no small part. The 1962 Immigration Act introduced a voucher system which closely regulated the number of new workers admitted whilst allowing for the entry into Britain of the dependants of workers already settled. This allowed the population of New Commonwealth origin to increase to 1.2 million in 1971 and 1.5 million in 1981. Nevertheless the British case is interesting in that it foreshadowed the '*Gastarbeiter*-stop' of continental European countries by more than a decade.

Turning our attention away from Europe, the next biggest area for postwar labour migration is North America. Historically, as we have seen, the United States owed its very existence to the import of labour power: white colonists, African slaves, Chinese, Japanese and other Asians. The descendants of the Africans originally brought in to work the southern plantations eventually functioned as a source of cheap labour for northern industries: their mass internal migration transformed the racial character of cities like New York, Chicago, Detroit and Philadelphia during the first two-thirds or so of the 20th century. Foreign migrants also flowed in. Rising labour demand during the 1940s led to the Mexican *bracero* programme whereby labour from the USA's southern neighbour was recruited and given certain guarantees as regards employment and living conditions. However, what started as a wartime emergency measure lasted for over twenty years as an effective system for procuring cheap labour for the USA economy. Between 1960 and 1978 about 7 million immigrants legally entered the USA. One-third of them came from Latin America, half from Mexico. By the early 1980s the number of migrant workers employed in the USA was reckoned to be 10 million. Latin America, southern Europe, the Caribbean and several countries in South and East Asia (India, the Philippines, Vietnam, South Korea) were the main source regions in an evolving migrant supply system that displays as complex and flexible a morphology as that of Western Europe (Salt, 1989).

Illegal immigration has long been a major problem for the United States' authorities. Today the country almost certainly has the biggest problem of illegal immigration in the world, with estimates of the number of illegal immigrants present ranging up to 12 million. In the 1950s for every *bracero* who entered legally another four immigrants entered illegally. The illegals became known as 'wetbacks' because many had entered by swimming across the Rio Grande which forms much of the border between the United States and Mexico. Illegal migration is often produced by the juxtaposition of rich and poor countries. The boundary between the southern United States on the one hand (especially its rich state of California) and Mexico and the Caribbean on the other is the sharpest divide between prosperity and poverty in the world. Small wonder that it has been crossed by so much clandestine human traffic! Three-quarters of the illegal entrants come from Mexico and the rest from other Central American states to the south, from Colombia, and from Caribbean countries like Haiti, the Dominican Republic and Cuba. The majority find work as domestics and agricultural labourers.

Canada too has been a country of mass labour migration since 1945, although unlike the United States it has no source of cheap labour on its doorstep. In the early postwar years nearly all entrants were Europeans: British, German, Dutch and Italians. The introduction of a non-discriminatory points system for screening migrant applications in the late 1960s opened the door to non-Europeans. The main sources in the 1970s were Jamaica, India, the Philippines as well as southern Europe (Italy, Portugal, Greece, Malta). Throughout the postwar period family entry was encouraged and immigrants were seen as future Canadian citizens. In 1986 about 36 per cent of the Canadian population were regarded as of immigrant origin (i.e. non-British, non-French, non-Native). Although Canada is one of the few

advanced countries to proclaim multiculturalism and to legislate
vigorously against racial discrimination, informal discrimination and
even attacks against blacks, Asians and Native People grew in
frequency during the 1970s and 1980s (Castles and Miller, 1993, pp.
74, 200).

Even more than Canada, Australia is affected by geographical
remoteness from potential sources of immigrants, making it difficult
for the country to evolve a rotational system of temporary labour
migration like Germany or Switzerland. Also like Canada, Australia's
early postwar immigration sources were overwhelmingly European,
political and racial attitudes militating against the use of more local
supplies in Polynesia and South-East Asia. Australia's immigration
policy was dominated by strategic demographic considerations
summed up in the slogan 'populate or perish'. Hence the population,
only 7.5 million at the end of the war, was to be boosted by 'racially
acceptable' stock from Britain and (when the British supply was
insufficient) the rest of Europe. By the 1950s Italians, Greeks and
Maltese were the largest groups of immigrants to Australia. Non-
Europeans were kept out by the racially explicit 'White Australia'
policy which remained in force until the late 1960s. By this time the
southern European source was also drying up and recruitment widened
to Yugoslavia and Latin America. Relaxation of the White Australia
policy, combined with refugee obligations, allowed new flows in from
Vietnam and Lebanon, as well as migrants from the populous Asian
countries where push pressures for emigration were strong, such as
India, Malaysia and the Philippines.

There has been a close relationship between immigration and
economic growth in Australia. Between 1947 and 1973 Australia's
labour force grew faster than that of any other Western country: half
of this growth was accounted for by immigrant workers. By the 1970s
Australia's manufacturing industry was so heavily dependent on
immigrant labour that factory jobs were automatically known as
'migrant work'. Foreign labour thus drove the Australian economy
forward, but when that economy faltered, immigration was quickly cut
back. Hence the last 20 years has seen a continual see-sawing of the
immigration figures. The recession of the early 1970s cut immigration
to about 50,000 per year, less than half the level of the 1950s and
1960s. It grew again to an average of 100,000 per year in the late

1970s but was cut to 60,000 in the recession of the early 1980s; then it grew once more to about 140,000 per year in the late 1980s before falling yet again in the recession of 1991-92 (Castles and Miller, 1993, pp. 74-5, 83-4).

I next consider a migration pole which is fundamentally different from the industrially-driven postwar labour migration networks of Western Europe, North America and Australia. The Middle Eastern migration system is based on the economic potential generated by a single commodity – oil – and is focused on the Gulf region and to a lesser extent Libya. After the initial discoveries in the 1930s, the oil economies developed quickly during the 1950s and 1960s on the basis of labour drawn in from the Middle East region, so that by 1970 about 85 per cent of the 750,000 migrant workers in the Gulf and Libya were from other Arab countries such as Egypt, Tunisia, Jordan and the Yemen. Accelerated economic growth after the massive oil price increases of 1973-75 involved the recruitment of labour from a wider arena – Turkey (including unemployed returned *Gastarbeiter*), Sudan, India, Pakistan, the Philippines and Korea. Virtually the entire Asian region from the Mediterranean to the Pacific has been transformed into a source of labour recruitment for the sparsely peopled countries privileged with oil.

Immigrant labour in the oil states has been channelled into a rather narrow range of sectors, particularly infrastructural development (roads, airports, military bases, health centres, schools, universities etc.) and, more recently, services and some industries. Capital-rich and labour-poor, the Arab oil-exporting countries have lacked the indigenous labour required to execute these projects and use up the colossal oil revenues which contribute as much as 90 per cent of their states' budgets. Multinational involvement with the oil industry and the need to recruit expert technical and managerial staff have also led to the temporary installation of high-status workers from North America and Europe.

Thus to small indigenous populations (4.6 million in Saudi Arabia, 2.3 million in Libya, 500,000 in Kuwait, 200,000 in Bahrein and 45,000 in Qatar – figures from the mid-1970s) have been added about 3 million foreign workers. In Kuwait, Qatar and the United Arab Emirates there are actually more foreigners than natives. And therein lies one of the perceived dangers as seen by the immigration coun-

tries. Hence immigration has been tightly monitored and institutionalized with family migration (except for Western experts) prohibited,
even for fellow-Muslims. Increasingly, labour migration has been
organized and packaged by contractors from countries like Turkey and
Korea. In this way contact with the indigenous Arab population is
further minimized. Such workers, brought in on annual contracts from
the cheapest regions of the global labour market, housed in high-
density, fenced-off hostel compounds, have almost no identity with the
place or the economy they work in.

Smaller-scale regional labour migration systems focus on South
Africa and the 'southern cone' of South America, where Argentina is
the main magnet. One estimate for 1990 (Segal, 1993, p. 48) gives 2
million immigrants in Argentina, mainly from Paraguay (800,000),
Bolivia (700,000), Chile (300,000) and Uruguay (200,000). Most are
farm labourers and construction workers. However, as farm mechanization has progressed and as the strength of the Argentine economy has
waned, the rates of inflow have fallen off during the 1980s.

South Africa's highly organized migrant labour system has some
parallels with that of the Gulf (males only, strict rotation, hostel
accommodation, link to mineral extraction) but it also has unique
features. The roots of the system lie in the colonial period when most
of southern Africa was under British rule. The exploitation of rich
mineral resources (gold, diamonds and coal) needed abundant labour.
Most of the legally recruited miners are from Lesotho, Swaziland,
Botswana, Malawi and Mozambique, adjacent poor countries. South
Africa's recruitment of migrant labour illustrates well the link between
migration and broader patterns of economic and political dependency.
Lesotho and Swaziland are respectively completely and largely
surrounded by South African territory. In addition to this geographical
entrapment, poverty and the absence of alternative employment
opportunities make reliance on opportunities in the South African
mines virtually the only livelihood for much of the population, despite
the high health and accident risks involved. By 1973 nearly 80 per
cent of the black miners in South Africa were foreigners. Since then
the situation has changed and this proportion has halved. Political
tensions with the surrounding states have led to the 'internalization' of
sources of labour within the newly-fashioned black 'homelands' –
created deliberately as segregated labour reserves by the South African

government under the system of apartheid and racial exploitation. This internalization seems set to continue in the post-apartheid era since the homelands face worsening poverty and unemployment (Castles and Miller, 1993, pp. 143–5).

Japan appears to be the exception to the need for major centres of industrial capitalism to recruit cheap foreign labour: in order to guard against population overcrowding and preserve ethnic and cultural homogeneity, Japan has resisted large-scale labour imports. Closer inspection reveals that this exceptionalism is only partly true. Korean migration during the present century has been considerable. Before 1939 Korean labour migration to Japan was an expression of Japanese colonialism with anti-industrialization policies and dispossession of the Korean peasants. During World War II the process became one of forced recruitment for the Japanese war economy, and the number of Koreans in Japan rose to nearly 2 million in 1944. Today there are some 700,000 Koreans in Japan, most of them descendants of these forced labour migrants and a source of cheap labour themselves. They are not well treated by the Japanese authorities, receiving no un-employment, sickness or pension benefits from the state (Potts, 1990, pp. 152–3).

The pressures for migration to Japan from nearby labour-surplus countries are considerable. Although the Japanese Labour Ministry claims that the economy has enough Japanese labour to sustain it, there are serious locational and skill mismatches, whilst falling fertility is decreasing the number of new entrants to the labour market. Labour shortages have emerged since the early 1980s. Young, highly-educated Japanese are unwilling to take factory jobs, and there is little scope for further rural–urban migration or for increasing the rate of participation of females in the labour force. The official policy is to increase investment overseas – i.e. to export jobs rather than import labour – but there are limits to this since many low-grade jobs in services and construction cannot be exported. Government strategy stresses the strict control of illegal immigration and limits immigration to those with special skills. However, chinks in the armour of 'Fortress Japan' are now appearing. In 1990 employment of unskilled foreigners of Japanese origin was permitted, leading to a rush to recruit the descendants of Japanese migrants to Brazil. Schemes for bringing in students and trainees from abroad have become cloaks for illegal worker migration. Other illegals arrive as tourists and overstay: like their counterparts in Europe and America they are concentrated in jobs which are dirty, dangerous, insecure and low-paid. The illegal migrants come from many Asian countries but especially Korea, the Philippines, India and Pakistan. Their number was estimated to be 480,000 in 1991, with the likelihood of an explosive increase in the 1990s (Prasai, 1993). The reasons for this are not hard to see, with Japan's average per capita income of US $17,000 contrasting with that of US $550 for the Philippines, for example.

POST-INDUSTRIAL MIGRATIONS, ECONOMIC RESTRUCTURING AND GLOBALIZATION

The discussion now moves on to examine some of the intricate relationships between international migration and contemporary globalization, in particular the restructuring of economic activity which started in the 1970s and is still going on today. We shall retain our primary focus on Europe, in order to preserve continuity with the earlier discussion on labour migration, but also touch briefly on other world areas. Globalization and economic restructuring are complex processes whose characteristics are only now beginning to be explored. Here I will concentrate on the extent to which migrants are mainly drawn into, but also sometimes contribute towards, the reshaping of economic activities and global relations. But first, how has economic restructuring affected the *Gastarbeiter* who, in most cases, are no longer 'guestworkers' but permanently settled immigrants?

The worker migrations of the 1950s, 1960s and early 1970s were very much mass phenomena: millions of more or less homogenous workers mass-migrated from rural areas of poor countries to take jobs in industries in the prosperous countries where they contributed to the mass production of goods for mass consumption (Fielding, 1993). Since in many cases they were specifically recruited to staff these enterprises it is not surprising that they should be disproportionately affected by the crisis and collapse of many of these mass-production industries. In Britain, for example, the decline of a whole variety of manufacturing industries – iron and steel, engineering, cars, textiles

– has nearly always impacted negatively on immigrant workers from Ireland, the Caribbean and South Asia. In other sectors it was less the decline of the industry which was important and more the changing character of the production process with machines, computers and robots displacing assembly-line labour.

In many cases the displaced workers are of an age and background which makes it difficult for them to retrain for other jobs, and so unemployment levels of most ethnic groups have risen significantly above the host country averages for Britain, France, Germany, and so on. Return migration is not an option for most because of the length of time they have been abroad and the fact that they have children and even grandchildren who have been born and reared abroad. Some unemployed migrants have been wary of leaving in case they forfeit their right to re-enter. Moreover their home countries may still have little to offer them in the way of work and a livelihood. Such people are the victims of an international system of which they were made part and from which they cannot escape; criticism of their unemployment by the host societies merely adds insult to injury.

Changes in the global economy in the post-*Gastarbeiter* era have tended to polarize labour demand into high-skill and low-skill categories. This polarization also reflects an emerging duality between a *primary labour market* of well-paid, secure and pensionable jobs and a *secondary labour market* of poorly-paid, insecure and often part-time employment. Migration processes are affected accordingly, so that the skill profile of today's international migrants tends to reflect the polarity between highly-trained professionals, scientists and technicians on the one hand and low-grade casual, flexible service labour on the other (Sassen, 1988).

One of the clearest expressions of the globalization of economic life, and of labour markets in particular, is the rapid growth of skilled international migration – a new breed of executive nomads who, whilst quantitatively much less important than the mass labour migrations of the past, nevertheless wield enormous influence over the functioning of the global economy.

The growth of world trade and the international expansion of business have produced a well-developed international market for skilled and highly-educated labour. This market is highly structured or 'segmented' – differentiated by increasing specialization and refinement of technical and professional qualifications. Most of the migration of the highly skilled takes place amongst the advanced capitalist countries and consists of relatively balanced two-way exchanges between pairs of countries in Europe or with Japan or North America. It is facilitated by improved transport and communications, especially between the key nodal cities of the world economy. Some of this executive migration actually takes place within the labour markets of multinational companies who for reasons of business strategy, career planning or trouble-shooting, shift their high-status employees amongst the various countries they operate in. Since the end of the war multinational firms have had a steadily growing importance in the European and world economies. This importance has accelerated greatly in the last 15 years, particularly in some sectors such as banking and finance, accountancy and international business services. Many multinationals have complex locational hierarchies with different functions – management, research and development, main manufacturing base, branch plants, raw materials sourcing, and so on. – located in different countries and the need to constantly move staff amongst the various locations in the corporate hierarchy. Other skilled movement is stage-managed by recruitment agencies specializing in particular regions of the world or in occupational sectors like accountancy, economic planning, engineering and so on.

Obstacles to the movement of highly-skilled migrants are much less than for low-skill migrants. Special entry regulations and work permits have been introduced to facilitate their movement. Indeed some countries, such as Australia and Canada, have actively courted skilled and professional personnel, recognising their importance in improving the quality of their labour forces. Footballers, entertainers and artists are also able to relocate quickly and easily to most countries of the world.

John Salt predicts that the phenomenon of skilled international migration will increase further as companies become ever more market-oriented in their business activities and as European integration expands and deepens (Salt, 1992). However, he also points out that because of the expense of training and relocation packages, some companies are beginning to decrease the costs of skilled international migration by 'localizing' their recruitment and use of labour by various forms of decentralization. Other companies are replacing migration placements by shorter-term business and training visits, blurring the boundary between migration and mobility. On the other hand the internationalization of higher education with programmes such as the 'Erasmus' scheme, which aims at 10 per cent of European students studying in another country, or the 'Tempus' scheme for East–West student and staff mobility within Europe, would indicate an increasing willingness in the future for highly-educated people to live and work abroad.

Not all skilled international migration takes the form of 'talent exchanges' amongst the advanced countries. Two other situations occur. The first is the move of technical and managerial experts from more to less developed countries as part of contract migration or aid and development policy. Often such a migrant is charged with setting up or managing a particular project, and training a cadre of local people to eventually take over the running of the enterprise. This type of high-status labour migration is of relatively long standing, and echoes elite core-to-periphery migrations discussed at the beginning of this chapter. The second is the reverse flow, or brain drain, which I have already briefly referred to. Brain drains often move along channels defined by former colonial links and may be tied to particular shortages of skilled personnel – for example the migration of Indian doctors and West Indian nurses to Britain. They often reflect high levels of intellectual unemployment in the country of origin whereby the education system has been expanded and distorted, often by colonial influences, beyond the capacity of the country to absorb its own graduates. India, Sri Lanka and Egypt are examples of countries with massive intellectual unemployment and long-established brain drains.

At the other end of the skill profile, world labour market trends, especially the restructuring of labour demand in major cities in advanced countries, have opened up new possibilities for low-status migrant workers, most of whom originate from the Third World. These opportunities are very different from the factory jobs offered to migrants a generation ago. Most of the new low-skill jobs are in the tertiary sector, many in the informal economy; but others are in agriculture where there may be a strong demand for seasonal labour. The very vulnerability and desperation of the migrants makes them attractive as workers. This is the secondary labour market of casual, part-time, insecure work where rates of pay are very low by developed world standards, no social insurance contributions are paid, and not too many questions asked. These waves of post-industrial, often clandestine migrants have affected the United States, Europe, Japan and the Gulf. In a labour market which is becoming progressively deregulated and flexible, with strong pressures to reduce labour costs, they provide a pool of casual workers available for virtually any low-grade job at any time at any place.

Not only are there new types of labour migration in the post-industrial world, but there are also new countries of immigration. Amongst the most notable of these are four southern European countries: Italy, Greece, Spain and Portugal. All were countries of mass emigration during the intra-European migrations of the 1950s and 1960s but then changed to net immigration during the 1970s and 1980s. Several factors account for these countries' changed migration status (King and Rybaczuk, 1993; Pugliese, 1993). Increasing prosperity, aided partly by their incorporation into the EC, is a powerful macro-economic factor. The combined role of the expanding informal sector and the tertiarization of the economy have also provided the setting for many low-grade work opportunities for immigrants in hotels, restaurants, hospitals, office-cleaning, domestic service, workshop industries, construction and seasonal farm labour. Lax entry controls have also encouraged the migration inflows. Migrants have come from a very wide range of source countries in Eastern Europe, North Africa, Asia and Latin America.

Summing-up from the southern European experience, and generalizing these changes in the nature of modern migration onto a wider canvas, we can make the following points about the character of migrations in the period of global economic restructuring (cf. Castles and Miller, 1993, pp. 8–9, 77–8). First, migrations are more *global* in scale and intensity, and the incorporation of more and more countries into the global migration system tends to mean that most countries are in receipt of migrants from a greater diversity of countries than in the past. Moreover, second, these migrants are of a greater *range of types* than in the past. They comprise, for instance, labour migrants seeking long-term economic improvement, commuting migrants who want short-term or seasonal work, refugees and asylum-seekers, brain-drain migrants and student migrants. Third, many of these types of migration, especially asylum-seekers, refugees and illegal immigrants, are *accelerating* from many parts of the world. This acceleration reflects the growing importance of push pressures to migrate as compared to the previous dominance of the pull factor of labour demand. Finally, there is the *feminization* of many current migration flows. Women are increasingly acting as independent agents in international migration; indeed some national flows, such as from the Philippines or Cape Verde to southern Europe, are overwhelmingly female.

CONCLUSION

A summary of the history of labour migration in one chapter is from the theoretical and methodological points of view a hostage to fortune. Is there such a creature as the universal and timeless labour migrant? As I pointed out in the introduction, historians tend to work on parochial case-studies in which the theoretical stances or implications are rarely spelt out. Quantitative studies of migrant flows – either those which are purely descriptive or those which are analytical, perhaps involving model-building – are similarly often bereft of explicit ideology. If there is an ideology it is often a kind of hidden positivism or neoclassical economic base. Yet elements of universality in our study of migrant labour are observable. This may be purely a semantic point, but the very existence of the term 'labour migration' and its wide application across time and space must imply a degree of common experience.

What are these common experiences? The following points can be drawn out of, and developed from, the previous account.

First, labour migration has fulfilled a historic role of facilitating development in the areas of recruitment; rather less in the areas of departure. These labour supplies are often drawn initially from rural hinterlands within the country, and subsequently from foreign sources. Thus in 19th-century Europe a basic precondition for industrialization was the existence of labour reserves in rural areas; peasants and artisans flooded into towns, creating mass currents of rural–urban migration. When these reserves ran dry, foreign labour was used.

Comparing 19th-century transatlantic migration with postwar intra-European labour migration Kindleberger (1965) found that 'in both cases cheap labour fed economic growth by holding down wages ... and maintaining high rates of profit, investment and expansion'.

Second, migrant labour has a close relationship with the production of particular commodities. Under slavery and indenture, sugar was the prime example, but tea, coffee, cotton, rubber and many other specialized plantation crops have been the cause of labour migrations since the onset of slavery. In Europe, too, the specialized cultivation of certain crops with heavy seasonal labour demands (wheat, grapes, potatoes etc.) has generated seasonal labour migrations since the 17th century, some of which were international in scale. Then the industrial era brought new economic activities which had an insatiable appetite for migrant labour: railway building, mines, steelworks, automobile plants and many more.

A third generalization of an economic nature is that most modern labour migrations can be seen to correspond to 'developmental gaps' between countries and regions (cf. Hoffmann-Nowotny, 1978). Within modern Europe the case of Italy best exemplifies interregional mass labour migrations – from the south to the north of the country during the 1950s and 1960s. On the international plane highly developed countries are able to use developmental gaps to recruit workers from less prosperous countries. The populations of the less fortunate countries are thus regarded as a kind of reserve labour force by political authorities as well as by entrepreneurs and by broad segments of the native work forces. Spatial proximity has often played a crucial role in the construction of supply and demand relationships for labour – thus Britain has drawn extensively on the Irish labour reserve, Sweden on Finland, Switzerland on Italy, the United States on Mexico, and so on.

The development gap theory can, in certain countries, produce simultaneous emigration and immigration. Southern Europe experienced this in the 1970s and 1980s. This can be explained by two sets of circumstances. First, regional disequilibria within countries can generate emigration from one region (such as the Italian Mezzogiorno) and immigration to another (Rome and the north of Italy). Second, the segmentation of the labour market, both internally and inter-nationally, can produce two migration currents which are complementary rather than competing: emigrants from Italy and Spain go abroad for industrial or professional work; immigrants from the Third World perform tasks (domestic service, seasonal farm labour) which are rejected by local people.

However, to fully understand labour migrations we must add in the social context. This is my fourth concluding point. In the words of Kingsley Davis (1974, p. 96), 'Whether migration is controlled by those who send, by those who go, or by those who receive, it mirrors the world as it is at the time'. But the social embeddedness of migration can be quite complex. On a macro-scale labour migrations reflect the international social relations of capitalist production. Regarding social structure, migrations both reflect and change both of the societies they impact upon, that of departure and that of destination. Moreover, migrants' class positions may be completely different in the societies of origin and destination. In the receiving society migrant workers are often accorded a kind of 'underclass' status. On the other hand they might have originated from respectable artisan or middle peasant classes in their home societies; and they might return as highly-esteemed *nouveaux riches*.

Fifth, for the sending societies, and especially their ruling elites, the safety-valve theory has frequent relevance. From a regulationist framework the ability to 'disgorge' surplus population, especially unemployed workers who might disrupt the social order, has obvious attractions. Over the longer term of economic strategy, Europe's ability to 'export' surplus population through colonial settlement migrations was a contributory factor in creating the right mix of factors of production for sustained economic growth per capita, especially in the 19th century.

Another theme which is recurrent, even if it was only mentioned in passing in a couple of places, is the way in which the management of labour migration gives rise to an intermediate class. Under the colonial system of forced and semi-forced labour transfer, three groups drew benefit: the African chiefs and Indian and Chinese headmen who handled the supply side; the traders and transporters, who usually belonged to the colonial power; and the overseers and foremen who supervised the plantation or mine workers at their destination (Marks and Richardson, 1984, pp. 12–13). More recent historical parallels would include the Chinese migration syndicates operating on the west coast of America, the Italian *padrone* system of migrant control and sponsorship, and the contemporary smugglers who arrange for illegal immigrants to enter Western Europe.

Seventh, the long history of migration makes cultural and racial hybridization a deeply historical process. Many places of immigration, such as port cities and major metropolitan centres, have received multiple pulses of immigrants, either simultaneously or layered through time. Multicultural diversity inevitably results, either through intermarriage and fusion or through preservation and separation. The legacies of past migrations are nowhere more clearly seen than in former colonial societies where 'plural societies' survive as amalgams of racially distinct groups bound together by a hierarchical division of labour.

Where patterns of migration have been long established, as in Ireland or the Caribbean, migration may have such an all-pervasive influence that it becomes a national institution and part of the collective psyche of the people. The structure of social and national life may become completely dominated by migration, with a large part of the population consisting of returned migrants. In the Caribbean migration has been so institutionalized that it has become the primary socio-economic resource of the islands and a referent for the most dominant cultural symbols from literature to folklore (Patterson, 1978).

Finally, labour migration has, through time, become less 'free'. In fact people are less free to migrate internationally in the 1990s than they were in the 1890s. In the modern era of globalization, capital's freedom to migrate internationally is not matched by equal freedom of movement by labour. Moreover, some people are freer to migrate than others. Regimes of migration control filter out 'desirable' migrants (those with education, skills in demand, and from a similar cultural background) from those regarded as 'undesirable'. Hence modern labour migrations are becoming increasingly selective.

REFERENCES

Baines, D. (1991), *Emigration from Europe 1815–1930,* London: Macmillan.

Barth, G. (1964), *Bitter Strength: A History of the Chinese in the United States, 1850-1870*, Cambridge, Mass.: Harvard University Press.

Beijer, G. (1969), 'Modern patterns of international migratory movements', in J.A. Jackson (ed.), *Migration*, Cambridge: Cambridge University Press, pp. 11–59.

Bodnar, J. (1985), *The Transplanted: A History of Immigrants in Urban America*, Urbana: Indiana University Press.

Bowen, E.G. (1966), 'The Welsh colony in Patagonia 1865–1885: a study in historical geography', *Geographical Journal*, 132(1), pp. 16–31.

Castles, S. and Kosack, G. (1973), *Immigrant Workers and Class Structure in Western Europe*, Oxford: Oxford University Press.

Castles, S. and Miller, M.J. (1993), *The Age of Migration*, London: Macmillan.

Cohen, R. (1987), *The New Helots: Migrants in the International Division of Labour*, Aldershot: Avebury.

Corrigan, P. (1977), 'Feudal relics or capitalist monuments? Notes on the sociology of unfree labour', *Sociology*, 11(3), pp. 435–63.

Curtin, P.D. (1969), *The Atlantic Slave Trade: a Census*, Madison: University of Wisconsin Press.

Curtin, P.D. (1989), *Death by Migration: Europe's Encounter with the Tropical World in the Nineteenth Century*, Cambridge: Cambridge University Press.

Davis, K. (1951), *The Population of India and Pakistan*, Princeton, NJ: Princeton University Press.

Davis, K. (1974), 'The migrations of human populations', *Scientific American*, 231(3), pp. 93–105.

Denoon, D. (1984), 'The political economy of labour migration to settler societies: Australasia, Southern Africa, and Southern South America, between 1890 and 1914', in S. Marks and R. Richardson (eds), *International Labour Migration: Historical Perspectives*, London: Temple Smith, pp. 186–205.

Du Toit, B.M and Safa, H.I. (1975), *Migration and Urbanization*, The Hague: Mouton.

Ehrlich, A.S. (1971), 'History, ecology and demography in the British Caribbean: an analysis of East Indian ethnicity', *South-Western Journal of Anthropology*, 27(2), pp. 166–80.

Eltis, D. (1972), 'The traffic in slaves between the British West Indies colonies, 1807–1833', *Economic History Review*, 23(1), pp. 55–64.

Engels, F. (1962), *The Condition of the Working Class in England*, Moscow: Foreign Languages Publishing House.

Fagan, B.M. (1990), *The Journey from Eden: the Peopling of Our World*, London: Thames and Hudson.

Fielding, A.J. (1993), 'Mass migration and economic restructuring', in R. King (ed.), *Mass Migrations in Europe: the Legacy and the Future*, London: Belhaven Press, pp. 7–18.

Gemery, H.A. (1980), 'Emigration from the British Isles to the New World 1630–1700: inferences from colonial populations', *Research in Economic History*, 5, pp. 179–231.

Gilkey, G.R. (1967), 'The United States and Italy: migration and repatriation', *Journal of Developing Areas*, 2(1), pp. 23–35.

Graves, A. (1984), 'The nature and origins of Pacific Islands migration to Queensland, 1863–1906', in S. Marks and P. Richardson (eds), *International Labour Migration: Historical Perspectives*, London: Temple Smith, pp. 112–39.

Grigg, D.B. (1980), 'Migration and overpopulation', in P. White and R. Woods (eds), *The Geographical Impact of Migration*, London: Longman, pp. 60–83.

Handlin, O. (1951), *The Uprooted*, Boston: Little, Brown.

Hoffmann-Nowotny, H.J. (1987), 'European migration after World War Two', in W.H. McNeill and R.S. Adams (eds), *Human Migration: Patterns and Policies*, Bloomington: Indiana University Press, pp. 85–105.

Hvidt, K. (1975), *Flight to America: The Social Background of 300,000 Danish Emigrants*, New York: Academic Press.

Jackson, J.A. (1963), *The Irish in Britain*, London: Routledge & Kegan Paul.

Kindleberger, C.P. (1965), 'Mass migration then and now', *Foreign Affairs*, 43(4), pp. 647–58.

Kindleberger, C.P. (1967), *Europe's Postwar Growth: The Role of Labor Supply*, New York: Oxford University Press.

King, R.L. (1976), 'The evolution of internationl labour migration movements concerning the EEC', *Tijdschrift voor Economische en Sociale Geografie*, 67(2), pp. 66–82.

King, R.L. (1992), *Italian Migration: The Historical and Geo-*

graphical Background, Bristol: University of Bristol, Centre for Medi-terranean Studies Occasional Paper 5.

King, R. and Rybaczuk, K. (1993), 'Southern Europe and the international division of labour: from immigration to emigration', in R. King (ed.), *The New Geography of European Migrations*, London: Belhaven Press, pp. 175–206.

Kloosterboer, W. (1960), *Involuntary Labour since the Abolition of Slavery: A Survey of Compulsory Labour throughout the World*, Leiden: E.J. Brill.

Knox, P. (1984), *The Geography of Western Europe: A Socio-Economic Survey*, London: Croom Helm.

Kondapi, C. (1951), *Indians Overseas 1838–1949*, New Delhi: Indian Council of World Affairs.

Lee, J. (1978), 'Migration and expansion in Chinese history', in W.H. McNeill and R.S. Adams (eds), *Human Migrations: Patterns and Policies*, Bloomington: Indiana University Press, pp. 20–47.

Lowenthal, D. (1972), *West Indian Societies*, Oxford: Oxford University Press.

Lucassen, J. (1987), *Migrant Labour in Europe 1600–1900*, London: Croom Helm.

MacDonald, J.S. and MacDonald, L.D. (1964), 'Chain migration, ethnic neighbourhood formation and social networks', *Millbank Memorial Fund Quarterly*, 42(1), pp. 82–97.

McNeill, W.H. (1978), 'Human migration: a historical overview', in W.H. McNeill and R.S. Adams (eds), *Human Migration: Patterns and Policies*, Bloomington: Indiana University Press, pp. 3–19.

Marks, S. and Richardson, P. (1984), 'Introduction', in S. Marks and P. Richardson (eds), *International Labour Migration: Historical Perspectives*, London: Temple Smith, pp. 1–18.

Neal, L. and Uselding, P. (1972), 'Immigration: a neglected source of American economic growth', *Oxford Economic Papers*, 24(1), pp. 68–88.

Newbury, C. (1975), 'Labour migration in the imperial phase: an essay in interpretation', *Journal of Imperial and Commonwealth History*, 3(2), pp. 234–56.

Park, R.E. (1950), *Race and Culture*, Glencoe: Free Press.

Patterson, O. (1978), 'Migration in Caribbean societies: socio-economic and symbolic resource', in W.H. McNeill and R.S.

Adams (eds), *Human Migrations: Patterns and Policies*, Bloomington: Indiana University Press, pp. 106–45.

Patterson, O. (1982), *Slavery and Social Death*, Cambridge,
Mass.:Harvard University Press.

Piore, M.J. (1979), *Birds of Passage: Migrant Labour in Industrial
Societies*, Cambridge: Cambridge University Press.

Portes, A. and Rumbaut, R.G. (1990), *Immigrant America: A
Portrait*, Los Angeles: University of California Press.

Potts, L. (1990), *The World Labour Market: A History of Migration*,
London: Zed Books.

Prasai, S.B. (1993), 'Intra-Asian labour migration', *Asian Survey*,
33(11), pp. 1055–70.

Price, C.A. (1969), 'The study of assimilation', in J.A. Jackson (ed.),
Migration, Cambridge: Cambridge University Press, pp. 181–237.

Pugliese, E. (1993), 'Restructuring of the labour market and the role
of Third World migrations in Europe', *Society and Space*, 11(5),
pp. 513–22.

Russel-Wood, A.J.R. (1982), *The Black Man in Slavery and Freedom
in Colonial Brazil*, London: Macmillan.

Salt, J. (1989), 'A comparative overview of international trends and
types', 1950–80, *International Migration Review*, 23(3), pp.
431–56.

Salt, J. (1992), 'Migration processes amongst the highly skilled in
Europe', *International Migration Review*, 26(2), pp. 484–505.

Salt, J. and Clout, H.D. (eds) (1976), *Migration in Postwar Europe:
Geographical Essays*, London: Oxford University Press.

Sassen, S. (1988), *The Mobility of Labor and Capital*, Cambridge:
Cambridge University Press.

Schrier, A. (1959), *Ireland and the American Emigration, 1850–1900*,
Minneapolis: University of Minnesota Press.

Scott, F.D. (1968), 'The great migration from Europe', in F.D. Scott
(ed.), *World Migration in Modern Times*, Englewood Cliffs, NJ:
Prentice-Hall, pp. 9–12.

Segal, A. (1993), *An Atlas of International Migration*, London: Hans
Zell.

Souden, D. (1984), 'English indentured servants and the transatlantic
colonial economy', in S. Marks and P. Richardson (eds), *International Labour Migration: Historical Perspectives*, London: Temple

Smith, pp. 19–33.

Spengler, J.J. (1958), 'Effects produced in receiving countries by pre-1939 immigration', in B. Thomas (ed.), *The Economics of International Migration*, London: Macmillan, pp. 17–51.

Thomas, B. (1972), *Migration and Urban Development: A Reappraisal of British and American Long Cycles*. London: Methuen.

Thomas, W.I and Znaniecki, F. (1918), *The Polish Peasant in Europe and America*, New York: Knopf.

Tinker, H. (1984), 'Into servitude: Indian labour in the sugar industry 1833–1970', in S. Marks and P. Richardson (eds), *International Labour Migration: Historical Perspectives*, London: Temple Smith, pp. 76–89.

Zolberg, A. (1978), 'International migration policies in a changing world system', in W.H. McNeill and R.S. Adams (eds), *Human Migrations: Patterns and Policies*, Bloomington: University of Indiana Press, pp. 241–86.

77 - 113

Global
R 23
F22
J 61

2 Economic Migration and the Sending Countries

Bimal Ghosh

CHANGING CONFIGURATION OF INTERNATIONAL MIGRATION

Issues of Definition: Identifying Sending Countries

The changing configuration of inter-country movements of people challenges many of the traditional concepts and definitions used in migration literature, including the classification of countries as migrant sending and migrant receiving. For a long time migration flows had been tacitly perceived to be uni-directional and the focus in migration literature had often veered towards the receiving countries.[1] The regulatory framework and policy perspectives of the latter provided the main reference for categorizing different streams of migration (settlement migration, contract labour migration, irregular movements, refugee flows and so on). The list of receiving countries was generally considered to be limited to Australia, Canada, New Zealand and the USA as permanent settlement countries and Western Europe as a receiver of temporary or contract workers. By and large, migration literature paid little attention to the movements of labour that had taken place between colonies during the period of slave trade (prior to 1850) and particularly under the regime of indented labour (1834–1937), and had made some of them important receivers of foreign labour. In the 1970s as the oil-exporting countries became important importers of contract labour following hikes in oil prices, they were added to the list of major migrant-receiving countries.

Against this background the emergence by the mid-1980s of southern European countries, notably Italy and Greece, as both sending and receiving countries was a novelty for many analysts, as reflected in the wide discussion of the subject in the years that followed.

But to-day such developments are hardly a novelty. An increasing number of countries – in East-Central Europe, in East and South-East Asia and elsewhere – are involved in both sending and receiving migrants, including labour migrants. A recent survey of 98 selected countries reveals that 24 of them were both *major* sending/emigration and *major* receiving/immigration countries; 31 were *major* sending countries and 43 were *major* receiving countries.[2] In the coming years more will become *major* sending *and* receiving countries at the same time, just as more of to-day's sending countries will have large numbers of foreign workers on their soil.

A related point to be noted is that much of the international migration continues to take place within the developing regions. Out of a total world stock of more than 100 million migrants (including refugees) between 60 and 65 million are in the developing countries, including the Gulf states (Table 2.1). Not surprisingly, many of the *major* sending countries as well as sending/receiving countries mentioned above are found in the developing regions. Even if the labour migrants are less concentrated in developing countries than migrants in general, the role of these countries as receivers of labour migrants cannot be insignificant. If labour migration is defined in a wider sense (to include all economically motivated flows as discussed below), the importance of their role is further enhanced.

The implication of this situation is that for a meaningful assessment of the consequences of labour migration sending countries should be grouped into different categories, making a distinction between countries that are major senders of migrants and those that are both major senders and receivers of migrants. The differentiation should also take into account the stages of development of sending countries, given that the migration flows have different implications for countries which are at different stages of development.

For the purposes of the present chapter, however, labour-surplus countries in developing regions and Eastern Europe are grouped together and broadly identified as migrant-sending countries and the

Table 2.1   *World's migrant population: distribution of stocks by major regions 1993*

Region	Million
Africa	22–26
(of which refugees)	(6.4)
Middle East, South & South-East Asia	17–21
(of which refugees)	(5.2)
North America	25–27
(of which refugees)	(1.3)
Europe	23–24
(of which refugees)	(3.2)
Central & South America	8–13
(of which refugees)	(0.1)
Oceania	4.5–5
(of which refugees)	(0.05)
Total	99.5–116
(of which refugees)	(16.4)*

* Difference in the total is due to rounding.

Notes:
1   Figures for Europe do not include persons in the former USSR and Yugoslavia who, as a result of political changes, nov live outside the country or their ethnic origin.
2   Figures for refugees, which refer only to those of concern to UNHCR, do not include Palestinian refugees (estimated at 2.5 million at mid-1991). Between December 1992 and December 1993 the total number refugees fell by some 1.5 million. Preliminary figures indicate that the number may have gone up again in 1994.
3   In 1994 the United Nations estimated that the number of international migrants in the world, including refugees, may have been in excess of 125 million. (See, for example, Programme of Action of the United Nations Conference on Population and Development, Cairo, September 1994.)

Sources: United Nations, *World Migrant Population: The Foreign-Born*, 1989; ILO, *International Economic Migration*, November 1993; OECD, SOPEMI, 1993; and UNHCR, *Populations of Concern to UNHCR: A Statistical* Overview, 1993.

capital-rich countries (including oil-exporting Gulf states and the newly industrializing economies, unless otherwise specified) are regarded as migrant-receiving countries.

Economic Migration by Choice and under Compulsion

Problems of definition and measurement also arise in connection with what is generally regarded as labour migration. Some 35 million workers are estimated to be currently working in foreign countries, world-wide. But the figure can be misleading for several reasons. First, many of the large numbers of persons who enter the receiving countries every year as tourists, students and refugees/asylum-seekers and are recorded as such in migration statistics subsequently take on regular and irregular jobs. But the change may not be recorded immediately or in all cases. Many others enter from the beginning as irregular immigrants and find employment in the informal sector or in the underground economy. Large-scale legalization of irregular immigrants can suddenly change the picture.

Second, problems of overlapping could arise in cases where foreigners entering through the family reunion or family formation channel soon join the labour market. In other instances, temporary (and some times repeated) visits of teams of professional managers, technicians and skilled and unskilled workers to provide services in an importing country, can be recorded as labour migration in the traditional sense, although, in reality, they may be more in the nature of trade-related temporary labour movements. Finally, considerable ambiguity seems to persist about whether migration related to invest-ment and creation of employment – as witnessed in such varied countries as Australia, Canada and Hungary – should be included under labour migration.

Viewed from the sending-country perspective, the situation is no less complex. Labour migration by definition is caused by economic factors and considerations. But a good part of contemporary migration – be it South–North, East–West or South–South – is propelled by mixed (economic and non-economic) motivation or composite factors. Individuals and families seeking to escape an oppressive political regime are also often the victims of economic discrimination and hardship, just as economically motivated migrants may become more desperate or anxious to move because of the fears of political turmoil and insecurity. Political and economic motivations in such cases tend to become interwoven. Objectively, too, political instability and violence have so often been found to bring the home economy to a standstill or to complete ruins, as witnessed by countries like Angola, Liberia, Somalia and Sudan. Conversely, many of the domestic political conflicts are sharpened by, or have their origins in, economic failures and injustices. As a result, the distinction between economic and political migration is becoming increasingly blurred (Ghosh, 1994).

A further complication stems from the fact that even when the migrants are clearly motivated by economic factors, they do not necessarily participate in the organized labour market or do not do so in a uniform manner – in either the sending country or the receiving one. Elsewhere, in discussing economic migrants I have tried to highlight the distinction between those who move for sheer economic survival and those who do so to improve their earnings and welfare (Ghosh, 1992; Utzua, 1981).

Survival migrants usually belong to the subsistence farm economy or to the amorphous urban informal sector in the sending country. For many of the survival migrants getting a regular job itself is equal to having gained a wage increase. In such a scenario the search for employment – or rather the search for basic economic security – becomes a more powerful factor in building up migratory pressures than inter-country wage disparities. As they leave the home country under compulsion they may not have valid residence and work permits, often hold marginal jobs or swell the ranks of irregular jobs in the underground economy of the receiving country. The process normally operates at the periphery of the organized sector, making it difficult to reach the migrants effectively through the regular labour market mechanisms and measures. Hitherto confined mainly to Africa, Asia and the Latin American/Caribbean region, the survival migrants are now outflowing to industrial countries. Given the immigration restrictions in countries of destination and their lack of means, many of the potential survival migrants may fail to cross borders, but they may nonetheless be impelled to move, contributing to irregular migration or disruptive population movements. Whether or not the actual movements take place, they constitute a potential source of instability.

The other category of economic migrants – who may be called mobility or opportunity-seeking migrants – tend to be more circumspect about the benefits and costs of migration before they actually leave the home country. For them the move is more a matter of choice than of compulsion. They are therefore more sensitive to the labour market signals and inter-country differentials in income and economic opportunities. In general, they would prefer to seek admission and employment in the destination country through the regular channels. Mobility or opportunity-seeking migrants are essentially the traditional labour migrants. The 'guestworkers' in West Europe, the contract workers in the Gulf states, and the transient professionals across the globe – are some of the examples. Much of the theoretical discussion on the economics of migration has so far concentrated on this category of migrants.

There could be situations where the distinction between two categories of economic migrants could be blurred – a sudden economic crisis, an environmental disaster or a political upheaval can turn a potential mobility migrant into a survival migrant. Conversely, with an improvement in their economic plight some survival migrants may eventually move into the category of opportunity-seeking migrants. Also, efforts to escape from extreme economic hardship and the quest for better opportunities could in some cases be closely intermingled. But the distinction remains important as an analytical tool, especially in the context of South–South and South–North migration. A discussion on economically-motivated migration will remain incomplete unless both these categories are covered: the term 'labour migration' is used in this chapter interchangeably with 'economic migration' in this wider sense.

THEORETICAL MODELS AND REALITIES OF MIGRATION

Under rigid and over-arching theoretical models the assessment of the effects of migration on the labour market and the economy of the sending (and the receiving) country is clear and straightforward. For example, under classical economic theories of migration as workers move from low-wage to high-wage countries, it ensures a more efficient use of labour and narrows inter-country wage disparities. For the sending country it implies less unemployment, rising wages and a boost for economic growth through access to inputs such as remittances and skills of returnees. By assuming that labour is perfectly mobile and homogeneous and fully employed and that there are no state interventions or externalities associated with migratory movements, these theories perceive labour migration as a self-effacing or self-stopping process. And since the individual's interest is supposed to fully coincide with national and international interests, classical theories stipulate that migration has all-round beneficial effects – for the sending and receiving countries and the migrants themselves. Under the neo-classical theories a degree of refinements is introduced in some of these hypotheses – for example, by differentiating between different types of labour and by recognizing that there may be both winners and losers in sending and receiving countries. But the basic, over-arching approach remains intact.

At the other extreme, the core-periphery conflict theories take a diametrically opposite view of the effects of migration. Since, according to these theories, migration takes place between economically and politically unequal units, it widens rather than narrows wage and income disparities, retards the economic development of sending countries and leads to the pauperization of their workers, while enhancing the interest of the receiving countries.

The realities of contemporary labour migration are, however, far more complex than implied in these deterministic theories. Neither the unitary view of the global economic and political forces underlying the conflict theories nor the over-arching approach of the classical/neo-classical theories seems adequate to capture all the complexities of contemporary migration or the full range of its benefits and costs. Rather than using a deterministic theoretical-ideological frame of reference, this chapter will follow an empirical approach in appraising the effects of migration on the sending countries.

EMIGRATION POLICIES, METHODS OF RECRUITMENT AND THE LABOUR MARKET

Emigration affects the labour market, including labour mobility, the production system and the economy of the sending country mainly through the selection of migrants, remittance flows and return migration. From the sending-country perspective recruitment, remittances and return – the three Rs – are thus often perceived as the high points in the migration process. Emigration policies of the sending country provide a convenient starting point to analyse these major aspects of inter-country migration; they play a particularly important part in influencing the selection and recruitment of migrants which in turn impinge on the level and composition of the emigrants, their skills and other personal and professional attributes.

Policy interventions by sending-country governments vary widely: they could reflect a relaxed, *laissez-faire* stance of the government, with minimal direct intervention; or they could be actively interventionist. The objectives of the interventionist policy could also diverge, ranging from restriction or outright prohibition to active encouragement of migration. Countries often seek additional support for their national policies on migration by entering into bilateral and plurilateral agreements, and the interaction between them could impact on the migration situation. There could also be spillover effects of regional and multilateral trade and economic cooperation agreements on the migration dynamics of sending (and receiving) countries.

The encouragement given by several eastern Mediterranean countries to labour emigration in the 1960s and early 1970s in order to enhance their development objectives is well documented. To-day a significant number of developing countries continue to do the same, although the nature of government intervention including the use of policy instruments and the extent of its control over emigration vary (Shah, 1994; Seccombe and Lawless, 1988). In the Asian region, for example, most sending countries including Bangladesh, India, Pakistan, the Philippines and Sri Lanka, have special public offices to facilitate labour migration and to protect the interests and welfare of migrant workers. Some sending countries, for example, Jordan, Indonesia and the Philippines, have encouraged labour migration with concomitant programmes of training to avoid depletion of human resources needed for national development.

A number of countries followed, in one stage or another of their development, a selective approach to emigration in order to preserve their human resources, while others opted for a more restrictive policy for the purpose. The experience with the restrictive policy introduced by Syria in the mid-1970s reveals the difficulties in enforcing such a policy. Although the emigration of professionals and civil servants was brought under greater control after 1979, the outflows of skilled and unskilled workers could not be stopped. The situation led Syria to promulgate a decree in 1980 granting amnesty to all unauthorized migrants if they returned to the country within six months. The restrictive policies in several other countries – for example a ban on emigration for employment introduced by the People's Democratic Republic of Yemen in 1973 – did not meet with great success (Seccombe and Lawless, 1988).

Past experience shows that similar difficulties often arise in implementing policies of selective restrictions; the attempts by the Algerian government in 1965–73 and by the Jordanian government in 1976–77 to regulate the quality of emigration are cases in point. For at least a certain period Tunisia was more successful in its efforts to select candidates for migration and prevent the departure of those required for national development. In the early 1970s as Tunisia announced a policy of active encouragement to labour migration it also sought to bring emigration under closer government control. In 1967 only 15 per cent of departures were controlled by the official agency, by 1972 it had risen to 77 per cent (Seccombe and Lawless, 1988).

Methods of Recruitment

When the labour markets in both sending and receiving countries are flexible and well organized and movements are unrestricted at both ends of the flow, intermediation does not present a major problem. But contemporary migration from labour-surplus countries rarely takes place under such circumstances.

For the sending country the segmentation of the labour market – exacerbated by the recent expansion of the informal sector, potential migrants' lack of access to reliable and updated information about conditions of entry and job opportunities in the country of destination and often ambivalent or ineffective government policies – complicates the process of recruitment. In the absence of other effective mechanisms social networks assume a particularly important role and in many cases serve as a semi-public service. Movements from Mexico to the United States provide a typical example of how social networks can link villages and towns in the sending country with the labour markets of the receiving country. The flow of information thus transmitted may be particularly useful since it is based on the practical experience of those already working and living in the receiving country.

In Africa initial emigration often takes place to countries about which the migrants already have some information, especially as regards job prospects, living conditions and possible social support through existing social networks; the latter are often reinforced by clustering of migrants from the same ethnic and cultural groups in particular residential areas or zones. This is followed by chain migration involving close relatives and friends, and ethnic kinship. The selection of the migrants at the family level remains primarily a household decision.

Although the system plays a useful role, it also suffers from the drawback that the information received by the potential migrants may be biased or partial, and not fully representative of the general situation in the destination country. Another problem lies in the fact that potential labour migrants in other areas of the sending country, not previously exposed to emigration, may not have access to such networks. And the unequal access can lead to excessive outflows from certain areas or communities, draining their human resources. In the absence of adequate mobility of labour, this could ultimately aggravate geographical imbalances in the country's labour supply.

In most sending countries in Asia, government agencies are generally involved in the recruitment of migrant workers, although private agencies, legal and illegal, and direct recruitment often play a more important part than public agencies in actual placement of workers. To illustrate, in 1993 in Bangladesh, Pakistan and Sri Lanka probably less than 2 per cent of workers depended on public agencies. With a somewhat different approach to labour export, the Republic of

Korea has traditionally exercised a good deal of influence on the movements by directly assisting the companies (employing Korean and non-Korean workers) to win project contracts abroad. China, which started following the practice in 1979, now has 123 international companies which act as officially approved legal entities to export labour (and construction) services; recent estimates showed that a total of some 89,000 Chinese workers were employed abroad under this arrangement[3] (Zhang *et al.*, 1992).

Both in Asia and North Africa private placement agencies have become a dominant force in migratory flows. Should these recruitment activities be placed within the structure of a regular enterprise, it could help the intermediation process in the international labour market and may facilitate inter-country trade in labour services. The latter approach could be particularly effective in 'packaging' labour and skill-intensive services for export purposes as is being done by an increasing number of developing countries, in line with the example of the Republic of Korea.

But when recruitment of potential labour migrants depends on informal private agencies and groups without effective supervision and monitoring and especially when migration is illegal and spontaneous, there could be serious abuses and exploitation of the migrants. The growth of organized trafficking, run by the syndicates in sending countries, often in collusion with their counterparts in countries of destination, has now reached such a high proportion that it could soon undermine the system of orderly migration. According to one rough estimate, in 1993 some 100,000–220,000 irregular migrants (including non-deserving asylum applicants) may have made use of the services of traffickers at least at some point of the journey to move into Western European states. Illegal trafficking, according to the same estimate, might have yielded for the traffickers a total income of US $5–7 billion in 1993 (Widgren, 1994).

Although illegal trafficking in migrants is not a new phenomenon, several factors account for its acceleration in recent years. These include: globalization and interpenetration of national economies, progress in transport and communication technology, relaxation of exit control resulting from the dissolution of the Warsaw Pact and of the Soviet Union and economic and political liberalization in a number of developing countries, including China. The more immediate reasons of course relate to the rising emigration pressure in sending countries and immigration restrictions in the receiving countries alongside their unmet labour demand in certain skills and industries.

In the receiving countries it is not just the workers' aversion to certain jobs – for example those perceived to be dirty, difficult and dangerous (the so-called 3D jobs) – which account for demand for foreign labour at the lower end of the wage structure but also the continued existence of the less competitive industries, many in the informal sector. They seek irregular and low-cost immigrant labour (alongside trade protection) in order to survive. The slow pace of industrial restructuring and segmentation of the labour market in the industrial countries are thus at least partly correlated to irregular migration from labour-surplus countries. The availability of such irregular and cheap migrant labour (in addition to other constraining factors) also inhibits the outflows of capital as foreign investment in labour-surplus countries.

Even when fraudulent practices are not involved, and migration is legal, the fees charged by the agents could be exorbitant. A survey made in Thailand of returned migrants a few years ago showed that the risk of being defrauded and the high cost of obtaining an overseas job discouraged many workers from migrating and inhibited the proper functioning of the labour market (Roongshivin, 1985). The same study showed that 95 per cent of those migrants who were in debt had to raise loans to finance the cost of obtaining the overseas job. A more recent report for Sri Lanka confirms the fraudulent practices of unscrupulous agents and the high cost of obtaining a permit to work abroad (Gulati, 1993). Reports on Chinese migrants seeking entry into the United States revealed that the agent's fees for each migrant could be as high as $20–30,000. A number of migrant-sending countries in Asia have laws regulating such fees, but their effectiveness remains limited.

EMIGRATION, EMPLOYMENT AND WAGES

Reduced unemployment in the sending country is generally regarded as one of the important positive contributions of migration – a consideration that has led, as already noted, many countries to encourage labour migration. An ILO/UNDP study revealed that in Pakistan migration had provided jobs equivalent to almost one-third of the incremental labour force during the country's Fifth Plan period, 1978–83 (1988). Another study estimated that emigration from the Republic of Korea in 1978–81 had reduced unemployment from 6.8 to 5.5 per cent (Kim, 1983). In Sri Lanka the emigration of some 60,000 workers a year in the early 1980s relieved unemployment when joblessness in the country had reached 15 per cent and the labour force was growing each year by about 140,000 (Korale *et al.*, 1985). There is also some evidence that circulatory flows of migration can reduce fluctuations in unemployment levels, although much depends on the pattern of labour demand in the receiving countries.

Labour outflows can clearly provide some relief from unemployment, especially in overcrowded areas. In situations of rising unemployment and falling living standards as recently witnessed in countries of Eastern Europe, they can also serve as a temporary safety valve against mass discontent. But if the sending country's structural problems remain unresolved and the demographic pressure continues, the contribution of emigration to alleviating unemployment on a country-wide basis or at the aggregate level is likely to be limited. There are several reasons for this. First, except in special cases emigration does not involve more than 1 or 2 per cent of a country's labour force – too small a proportion to make a veritable dent into large-scale unemployment. In the case of Sri Lanka, for example, although as a proportion of the net annual increment of the labour force the gross outflow of migrants is one of the highest in South Asia (roughly 86 per cent of the increment), 14 per cent of the labour force remained unemployed in 1990 (Gunatilleke, 1994).

A related point to be noted is that when migrants are drawn from among the non-participants of the country's labour force, as in the case of the many Sri Lankan women working as domestic help or in the export-processing zones abroad, emigration hardly alleviates existing unemployment. About 66 per cent of Sri Lankan women working in the Middle East had been non-participants in the domestic labour force prior to their migration (Athukorala, 1990).

Second, implicit in labour migration is a selective process that tends to cream best workers from the sending country. When recruitment is organized and undertaken at the behest of employers, the search for the most qualified candidates is unavoidable; screening at the time of renewal of contracts reinforces the rigours of selection. Even in the case of selection based on decision by the household or family heads (or, as in some instances in Africa, by clan elders), the more dynamic and enterprising members are likely to be the preferred choice. As the sending country thus loses some of its most innovative and enterprising workers, both future economic growth and creation of new employment can slow down.

Third, and related to the above, is the risk of economic dislocation that can result from labour outflows, especially when several types of them take place at the same time. Such dislocation can lead to loss of output and income and future employment; and these losses might in some cases be compounded by their negative spread effect resulting from inter-firm linkages and population redistribution within the country. Finally, migration may lead to the postponement of the structural changes needed to generate and sustain a process of dynamic and broad-based development, capable of creating new employment opportunities.

Empirical evidence in several labour-sending countries confirms the negative consequences of labour outflows on production and eventually on employment. In the Arab region, for example, emigration in the 1980s led to labour shortages in Jordan, Oman, Yemen and Egypt. In certain parts of Jordan 65 per cent of the agricultural workers were non-nationals; in Yemen children were filling some full-time jobs normally held by adults, and in Egypt emigration of construction workers led to a decline in productivity in that sector. In some countries, the existence of reserve supplies of rural labour prevented a fall in agricultural output but led to increased rural to rural migration. In still others, there was evidence of increased farm mechanization, reflecting a substitution of capital for labour. The picture, often partial, could however be conflicting. To illustrate, in the case of Egypt, one study showed that migration in the 1970s did not reduce unemployment from its earlier level of 11 per cent (Ibrahim, 1982). On the other hand, another study made three years later concluded that if new entrants were taken into account, potential unemployment may have been reduced as much as 75 per cent (Amin and Awny, 1985).

The divergent, if not conflicting, findings about the employment effects of migration are not surprising, given that most of these studies are country – or area – specific and generally have a short-term perspective. The social and economic characteristics and cultural factors that influence the employment effects of labour outflows have rarely presented a uniform pattern in different countries and areas of study; and even in the same country they often evolved over time. Isolating the effects of labour outflows from those of other concurrent socio-economic changes in the sending society is always difficult. The short-time perspective makes it even more difficult to capture the full impact of labour outflows on employment, especially the incidence of their spread or second-round effect, reinforced by the various inter-linkages involved. More robust methodologies are needed to overcome these difficulties.

Just as labour outflows can enhance mobility in the domestic labour force, it can also increase labour force participation (Smart, 1984). In a number of sending countries, including the Philippines, Indonesia and Sri Lanka, migration has stimulated increased participation of female workers in the labour force through a twofold process. First, as the departure of large numbers of male workers and consequent labour shortages in certain occupations open up new job opportunities for female workers, more women are induced to join the domestic labour force. Second, increased feminization of the labour force has also been partly the result of new demands in the international labour market for services such as nursing, domestic help, entertainment and secretarial assistance. In the Sahelian region of Africa, where tradition and religion had earlier combined to inhibit migration of women, economic hardships and family survival strategy have in recent years led women to participate in economic activities, leading to long-distance migration.

In theory, labour outflows should lead to a rise in real wages and a fall in profits in the sending country. The owners of capital will lose and workers staying at home will gain; the distribution of benefits between skilled and unskilled workers will depend on the skill composition of the migrant workers (further discussed below under skill migration). In practice, however, given the level of unemployment and underemployment in labour-surplus countries, the general level of wages may not actually rise. And yet, there have been many cases of rise in wages as a result of migration-related temporary labour shortages in specific sectors such as construction.

This was the case for example in the Republic of Korea where wages in the construction sector rose sharply between 1975 and 1980. In Pakistan, the Philippines and Thailand the wages increased at a higher rate than for other sectors, although it was difficult to determine the extent to which the increases were caused by labour outflows and by the higher demands of domestic construction. Similarly, in Sri Lanka, since the mid-1970s the wages for workers in occupations affected by migration – including heavy equipment operators, motor vehicle drivers, engineering technicians and maintenance workers – had risen faster than in other occupations.

Shortages of skilled labour in construction and transport sectors were particularly critical in the period 1978–82. Between 1978 and 1983 nominal wages in the construction sector, for example, rose by about 280 per cent and real wages by about 40 per cent, although part of the rise might well have been due to the high domestic growth of the construction sector (Gunatilleke, 1994).

Can labour outflows stimulate technological progress? Limited available evidence suggests that labour shortages in local areas resulting from emigration can induce positive technological change, including a more innovative and rational use of labour and other resources. On the other hand, as the experience in several African countries, including Burkina Faso, Lesotho, Mali and Malawi has shown, the departure of young and forward-looking adult males can make local communities less responsive to change, hindering techno-logical progress rather than helping it. Overall, much depends on the structure of local leadership, cultural mores of the community and the general pattern of skill migration and skill replacement in the country.

Skill Migration

From a theoretical point of view skill migration has several effects in the sending country. First, given the higher wages in the receiving countries it normally increases the incomes of migrants. Second, it raises the incomes of those skilled personnel left behind. Third, assuming that the skilled labour receives its marginal product, large-scale skill migration lowers the average incomes of the non-migrant population in the sending society. Finally, in the absence of any rise in average incomes, the redistribution of income in favour of the highly skilled leads to an absolute decline in the incomes of the low skilled. 'Brain drain' may thus lead not only to reduced national output but also to a deterioration of income distribution.

The realities surrounding skill migration in most labour-surplus countries are, however, far too complex to permit such rigid and clear-cut conclusions as suggested in theory. Not surprisingly, skill migration has been one of the most widely debated aspects of labour migration since the 1960s. It has been strongly argued that the selection process as discussed above tends to deprive the sending countries of persons of high human capital value and that few of them gain in skills while working abroad (further discussed below under Return Migration). An excessive outflow of skilled and highly skilled workers (including professionals and technicians), in the form of brain drain, has been under criticism especially from developing countries over more than three decades on the grounds that its negative effect on training, production and technological progress can ultimately lead a fragile economy to stagnation. More recently, a similar concern has sometimes been expressed in the context of actual and anticipated migration of skilled personnel from East and Central European countries.

These negative aspects of skill migration have also been put in an ethical context as it widens disparities between rich and poor nations. The poor countries and their taxpayers bear the costs of training and maintaining the potential migrants and the receiving countries reap the benefits. To illustrate the order of magnitude of the problem, between 1972 and 1985 four Asian sending countries – India, the Philippines, China and the Republic of Korea – lost more than 145,000 workers with scientific training to the United States alone (UNDP, *Human Development Report 1994*). The loss of the public investment made in their education cannot be negligible. A related criticism is that since, as already noted, the human capital embodied in labour often acts as a complement to capital and technology, skill migration tends to depress wages of unskilled workers; it thus aggravates poverty in the sending country (while increasing the productivity of the receiving country).

These criticisms are often highlighted by comparing the available stocks of human capital between industrial and developing countries. To take an example, industrial countries have 85 scientists or technicians and 19 university graduates for every 1,000 people. By contrast, developing countries, on average, have only nine scientists and one graduate per 1,000 (*The Economist*, 8 October 1994) – a situation that constrains rapid technological upgrading of their economies.

The main counter arguments, too, are well known. Since skill migration is the result, and not the cause, of lack of job opportunities the phenomenon may also be seen as 'brain overflow'. From this perspective, the movements actually reduce the supply–demand gap of skilled workers in the sending countries and ensure optimal allocation of unused human resources from which the world economy gains. The investment made for the education and training of skilled workers is more in the nature of a sunk cost than an actual cost for the sending country. Placing restrictions on their movements is not easy to enforce and harder to justify in view of the human rights considerations involved. And in any case that is not an economic solution, since the basic problem of using idle human resources remains intact. The only alternative solutions would be to reduce the supply of skilled workers by reforming the educational system or to increase the demand for skilled workers by raising the level of domestic and foreign investment and creating more job opportunities for them (which would, *inter alia*, call for investments in infrastructure and import of equipment and technology) in the sending country. An additional argument in defence of skill migration concerns, as already noted, the individual's freedom of movement and the right to market his/her talents freely to maximize job satisfaction and the financial reward.

Clearly, however, the cost of skill migration is high for a sending country which already suffers from skill shortages or when the skills are difficult to replace. This is the case, for example, for many countries in Africa, which as a region may have lost one-third of its highly skilled personnel in recent decades. Between 1985 and 1990 the region lost an estimated 60,000 middle- and high-level managers (UNDP, *Human Development Report 1994*). It can be particularly frustrating for a country when persons sent abroad for further training as part of human capital development effort fail to return, as has happened in a number of African countries, including Nigeria, The Gambia and Zambia. The situation is worse when the emigrating professionals have to be replaced by more expensive expatriates. Africa probably has 30,000 of such foreign experts to-day. The initial cost of skill migration could be compounded by a series of additional or second-round negative effects – the departure of highly skilled personnel impeding the on-the-job training of intermediary cadres or the absence of a talented engineer diminishing the possibility of increasing the value of an entire product through the quality of his/her design.

Although, compared to sub-Saharan Africa, the problem is less serious in most other developing regions, several Latin American and Caribbean countries are facing a similar problem. Even in Asia where most countries have a wider human resources base and some have launched special training programmes for skill formation or skill replacement, sectoral or occupational skill shortages resulting from emigration have occurred in many instances; and at least in some countries this has adversely affected skills' development programmes. In Pakistan, for example, the non-formal system for apprenticeship training in the building trade has been seriously undermined by the emigration of the most skilled craftsmen. In some sectors, such as power generation and construction, labour migration has caused production bottlenecks and wage inflation. At the peak of labour emigration to the Gulf states the loss of construction and engineering skills in Sri Lanka led to a decline in output and delays in project implementation schedules. The situation did lead to increased labour mobility but at the expense of the small firms which lost their workers to the larger enterprises, involving the transfer of training costs to the former (Korale *et al.*, 1984).

In Jordan, internal rural–urban migration partly filled the gaps created by the migration of highly skilled workers in the early 1980s, but (aside from the fact that the skill replacement may have taken place at lower levels of labour productivity) it created skill shortages in rural areas. Elsewhere, as in mines on the Black Sea coast of Turkey, skill migration led to a sudden worsening of safety conditions. On the other hand, sector-specific experience in several countries (including Pakistan and the Philippines) has shown that when skills can be rapidly replaced and the production process easily adjusted, the losses from skill migration could be insignificant (Fernandez *et al.*, 1987). Several proposals have been mooted to compensate the sending for their losses due to skill outflows. A number of sending countries have taken action for this purpose at the national level with varying degrees of success but little progress has been made at the global level, involving both sending and receiving countries.[4]

Skill Migration and Trade in Skill-Intensive Services

A line of approach that has remained relatively unexplored to attenuate the problem of brain drain concerns a trade-off between long-term or permanent skill migration and increased production and participation in trade by labour-surplus countries in skill- and knowledge-intensive services.[5] For a variety of reasons – historical, economic and other – labour-surplus countries have so far somewhat neglected the development of their services sector, including business and professional services. There has also been a general feeling that labour-surplus countries have little comparative advantage in the world market for service industries.

However, as the experience of industrial and newly industrializing economies demonstrates, the development of many of the producer and business services is vital for increased efficiency and competitiveness of the manufacturing and primary goods-producing sectors and indeed for the whole economy. Experience also shows that closer interlinkages between services and manufacturing sectors lead to further expansion of the services sector, alongside an upward swing of the economy. Increased emphasis on the development and efficient use of skill and knowledge-intensive services in labour-surplus countries would thus help faster economic growth and therefore there would be less pressure for them to migrate.

Furthermore, available balance-of-payments data suggest that many labour-surplus countries have a revealed comparative advantage in a number of skill- and knowledge-intensive services. They should be able to export a variety of skill-intensive services such as engineering, accounting, legal, management consulting, nursing, software development, and data entry and processing. Faster development of skill and knowledge-intensive services and their wider use in domestic economy as for the export market can thus reduce the pressure for skill migration in the form of brain drain from labour-surplus countries.

Although many of these services can be provided across borders by making full use of modern computer and telecommunication systems, some temporary movements of persons are often essential to facilitate the service transaction or complete the delivery of the service input in the importing country. The Uruguay Round General Agreement on Trade in Services (GATS), adopted in 1994, has opened up wider prospects of market access for trade in services, including trade-related temporary movements of persons as service providers. Since these movements are temporary and directly linked to specific transactions, the problem of causing a depletion of human capital, as implied in brain drain, does not arise in most cases. On the contrary, such movements can widen the knowledge and enrich the experience of skilled personnel and thus contribute to human capital development of the labour-surplus countries. The importing industrial countries can also gain as a result of easier access to these services at lower prices, while avoiding the problems, real or perceived, of permanent immigration.

Increased opportunities for labour-surplus countries to participate in trade in skill-intensive services, including better access to export markets through temporary movements of persons as service providers, could thus serve as a partial substitute for permanent or long-term migration.

Remittances, Investment and Economic Growth

Three categories of remittances are associated with labour outflows: transfers from workers abroad for one year or more; transfers resulting from cross-border labour mobility for less than one year; and flow of goods and financial assets directly linked to migration. In 1990 the developing countries had a total labour-related credit flow of about $46 billion; the net amount (adjusted against debits) amounted to nearly $37 billion (Table 2.2). (Contrary to the oft-quoted statement they do not dwarf the official development assistance commitment of about $53 billion a year).

Table 2.2 *Direction of labour remittance flows*

Region	1980	1981	1982	1983	1984	1985	1986	1987	1988	1989	1990
New workers' remittances											
Developing economies	20,110	19,325	19,239	19,444	20,461	19,387	21,650	24,195	24,251	27,958	33,737
Credit	25,336	24,698	24,682	24,787	24,882	23,444	25,420	27,898	27,990	31,884	38,599
Debit	5,225	5,374	5,443	5,343	4,422	4,057	3,771	3,703	3,740	3,926	4,862
Developed economies	(10,607)	(11,057)	(11,026)	(10,631)	(10,366)	(10,107)	(10,840)	(11,955)	(13,682)	(14,900)	(18,230)
Credit	3,760	3,210	3,140	2,923	2,846	2,941	3,455	3,877	4,274	4,626	5,213
Debit	14,367	14,268	14,166	13,554	13,211	13,047	14,295	15,832	17,956	19,526	23,442
Net migrants' transfers											
Developing economies	(147)	(176)	(189)	(197)	(145)	(94)	(46)	38	208	130	43
Credit	230	247	182	151	155	131	205	254	437	346	212
Debit	377	424	371	348	300	225	251	216	228	216	168
Developed economies*	1,092	1,385	1,195	1,156	936	804	1,264	1,779	2,507	3,400	3,326
Credit	1,946	2,281	2,098	1,957	1,908	1,807	2,323	3,261	4,088	5,197	5,225
Debit	854	897	903	800	972	1,003	1,059	1,482	1,581	1,797	1,899
Net labour income											
Developing economies	1,161	1,693	2,016	2,360	2,130	1,756	2,001	2,222	2,502	2,910	2,923
Credit	3,713	4,019	4,283	4,688	4,332	4,056	4,562	5,237	5,654	6,161	7,144
Debit	2,551	2,326	2,267	2,328	2,202	2,300	2,561	3,015	3,152	3,251	4,220
Developed economies*	(1,874)	(2,330)	(2,307)	(2,512)	(2,712)	(2,686)	(3,506)	(4,899)	(5,944)	(7,117)	(10,243)
Credit	7,366	6,632	6,999	6,733	6,403	6,642	8,909	10,872	12,317	12,670	14,748
Debit	9,240	8,963	9,306	9,245	9,115	9,328	12,415	15,770	18,261	19,787	24,992
Net total labour-related flows											
Developing economies	21,125	20,841	21,066	21,607	22,445	21,049	23,604	26,454	26,961	30,998	36,704
Developed economies	(11,389)	(12,003)	(12,138)	(11,986)	(12,141)	(11,988)	(13,082)	(15,074)	(17,119)	(18,618)	(25,147)

* All high-income economies, plus Saudi Arabia were classified as developed economies for the purposes of this table.
Sources: UNCTAD/World Bank (compiled from IMF and World Bank databases).

98

The actual amount of remittances, however, far exceeds the official figures as a large proportion of workers' earnings is often through non-official channels. An extreme case was that of Sudan where, according to one estimate, only 11 per cent of the remittances flowed through the official channels (Choucri, 1985).

Remittances have a significant impact on the economy and household welfare of many migrant-sending countries, although their effect on the labour market is mostly indirect and limited. Remittances obviously boost the earnings of the migrants' families, and since – unlike government-to-government aid – these transfers go directly to the final recipients, they can significantly promote welfare and human capital at the household level. The full amounts of transfer need not, however, be regarded as a net addition to the household budget or the sending-country economy. The opportunity cost of migration – the possible earnings forgone by the migrant in the home country – must also be taken into account (even in a labour-surplus country the marginal product of labour rarely falls to zero).

Remittances have improved children's education in some countries (e.g. Jordan, Thailand and the Philippines), while in others (e.g. Pakistan and the Pacific islands) they have contributed to better health and higher productivity of (non-migrant) members of the family by raising levels of consumption. They can also help develop social assets and facilities such as schools, and health centres, as was witnessed in certain emigration areas of Kenya, Lesotho, and some Sahelian countries. Migrants in the receiving country have sometimes been found to pool their resources and transfer them to their homeland for such purposes.

There is also wide agreement that remittances can provide valuable support to the balance of payments accounts, as exemplified by countries like Bangladesh, Burkina Faso, Egypt, Jordan and Morocco, and help economic development by providing foreign exchange for essential imports. Equally important, remittances can also help countries in tiding over temporary foreign exchange difficulties following trade liberalization, although it is doubtful whether they serve as the main determining factor in the policy reform itself, as some analysts have implied. The basic considerations propelling such policy changes often lie elsewhere.

The important caveat to these positive effects on balance of payments accounts is that remittances can lead to changing consumption patterns among remittance-receiving households, encourage increased consumption of imported goods and can thus add to the import bill.

The long debate on the micro-economic effects of remittances still continues. But much of the debate – for example, the question of whether and how much of the transfers is spent on consumption or used for productive investment – is wrongly focused and largely meaningless. Since remittances are a private transfer to the household budget, they need not be perceived as, or equated with, capital imports which are geared, directly and in full, to investment. True, remittances do not generally find their way into productive investment; but this should be considered only normal if, as has been found in a number of cases, the expenditure pattern of non-remittance-receiving households in the same income group reveals similar characteristics. The second point to be noted is that most of the earlier studies – which showed the consumption preference of remittance-receiving households – focused on the *proportional* distribution of remittance expenditure between different uses. More recent studies have revealed that, except for the lowest income groups, the household's marginal budget share for consumption is quite low.

Where the macro-economic environment is stable and other conditions are conducive to investments, remittances can raise the level of domestic investment. In the Republic of Korea, for example, a 10 per cent increase in remittances was estimated to increase total fixed investment by 0.53 per cent and GNP by 0.24 per cent (Abella, 1993). Data from five migrant-sending Asian countries revealed a positive statistical relationship between the rate of labour emigration (average yearly emigration as a ratio of total employment) and the rate of gross domestic savings, in the case of three of the five countries examined (Abella, 1993). Field observations on remittance expenditure in several African countries have shown that even in rural areas remittance-receiving families tend to take rational decisions under prevailing social and economic conditions and legal and financial systems.

A third important point is that the micro-economic effect of remittance expenditure needs to be analysed in a wider perspective, and not just in terms of its direct use for investment. Analyses of the dynamic macro-economic impact of remittance expenditure in, for example, Egypt, Greece and Pakistan have shown that the multiplier effect of such expenditure on GNP could be as high as 1:2 or even more. To put it differently, a remittance of one million Egyptian pounds would increase the country's national income by more than 2 million pounds (Glytsos, 1990; Kandil and Metawally, 1992; Nishat and Bilgrami, 1991).

In some countries remittances have been found to have an inflationary effect on goods and assets (such as land) whose supplies were inelastic; in some others the flows seem to have fuelled demand-pull and cost-push inflation in the consumer goods sector. But it was also found in a number of other countries (e.g. Turkey) that the remittances reduced inflation through essential imports such as spare parts and new machinery.

Clearly, remittances have a number of negative consequences. They entail an element of uncertainty in the migrants' family income just as they make remittance-dependent economies vulnerable to sudden external shocks. The budgetary strains caused in the migrant-sending countries following the unexpected repatriation of 2.8 million workers and their dependants, caused by the recent Gulf crisis, is a case in point. It has been suggested that the remittance dependence was largely responsible for the Salvadorian government to plead with the United States not to return large numbers of undocumented Salvadorian immigrants following the enactment of the US Immigration Reform Control Act of 1986 (Castillo, 1994). Also, excessive dependence on remittances as a means of earning foreign exchange to finance development in the earlier stage of industrialization could be self-defeating in as much as that this could delay the process of essential structural adjustment and policy reform.

Remittances and Social Change

Remittances are sometimes considered to weaken social cohesion and enhance income inequality . Some studies have shown that remittance income can produce markedly different standards of living and create distinct economic classes based on migrant status. Migrants from rural

Mexico holding United States' resident visas, for example, tended to monopolize scarce local resources – land, cattle, and commercial enterprises – strengthening economic asymmetry and social stratification (Rubenstein, 1992). Some studies in Asia have also shown that migration-related remittances can increase income inequality in the sending community. But the evidence seems to be inconclusive. Much depends on the income level of the migrant households. To the extent that migrants come from above average income households, remittances may exacerbate income inequality, as was found through studies in Egypt. However, when a poorer member of the sending society migrates, it can have a positive effect on poverty. In Egypt, when remittances were included in a recent estimate of household incomes, the number of poor households showed a significant decrease of 10 to 12 per cent (Adams, 1991).

Emigration can significantly change social and family structures and cultural values. Although these issues are outside the scope of the present chapter, it is important to note that many of these changes can also have a significant impact on production patterns, labour market trends and the demographic situation of the sending country. Research in an Egyptian village showed women left behind became more involved in cultivation, management of financial affairs and household decision-making (Khafagy, 1983). But the experience varies between and even within countries, depending on local circumstances. For example, in another Egyptian village it was found that male migration did not lead to any significant change in the productive roles of migrants' wives (Taylor, 1984). Elsewhere, as in the Yemen Arab Republic, it was found that female seclusion increased in the households of successful migrants.

In some African countries, emigration of male members of the family has enhanced the role of women in the family and in the production system, but it also led, if temporarily, to a fall in agricultural output. A study made in the Taiz province of the Yemen Arab Republic showed increased seclusion of women left in the care of male relatives (Mynitti, 1984). In some Caribbean countries male emigration did not lead to an active involvement of women in production because of legal and social constraints and may have led to a decline in smallhold farming.

Impact on family relationships can also vary widely. In Sri Lanka, for example, investigations among returnees showed that 99 per cent of males and 92 per cent of females were of the view that family relations had been strengthened (Gunatilleke, 1991). By contrast a study of 74 families in Jordan concluded that labour migration had a negative effect on family ties (Kamiar and Ismail, 1991).

The demographic effects of migration in the sending country also present a variegated pattern, influenced by the level of emigration, the nature of the outflows and a complex set of socio-economic variables. A high level of emigration can mean a moderate growth of population, despite continuing high fertility rates among the non-migrants. In the Caribbean, for example, net migration resulted in off-setting 52 per cent of the natural increase of the region's population during the period 1960–70. But the age selectivity of migration and the youth of the female emigrant cohorts can also accelerate the ageing of the local population, as happened in certain areas of Greece following substantial emigration to the Federal Republic of Germany. Should this lead to high dependency ratios, this could also imply an eventual fall in the fertility rate in areas of high emigration. The nature and composition of the flows could be another factor to affect the fertility rate among the non-migrants. In Jordan, for example, the selectivity of migration favouring the educated and high-level professional groups with a lower fertility rate may have meant a higher than average level (calculated for total population) of fertility among the non-migrants remaining in the country.

BENEFITS OF RETURN

The sending country can reap the benefits of return migration in the form of an increase in the stock of its human capital. However, this would happen only when three conditions are met: migrants return home with new skills that are more productive than what they would have learned at home; the skills learned abroad are relevant to the needs of the home country; the returnees must have the willingness and the opportunity to use the skills upon return.

The promises of return migration, however, often remain unfulfilled.

Highly skilled workers generally have more opportunities to acquire additional skills and knowledge than the less skilled ones. They have easier social acceptance in the receiving country and more easily overcome the difficulties of social and cultural integration. They are thus likely to be more successful and productive in the host country and have less compelling reasons to return.

Data on return migration in several countries, including Greece and Turkey, confirm that more skilled and successful migrants are less likely to return. A significant proportion of those who return cannot therefore be expected to be a source of new skills and knowledge.

Several studies in other regions also fail to show any significant upgrading of skills for the majority of the migrants working abroad. In one case involving migrants from Bangladesh to the Gulf states it was found that less than one per cent of the workers held jobs requiring higher skills than they had possessed before departure. Skilled and semi-skilled migrants have also been found to accept lower-level positions implying downward occupational mobility and downgrading of skills. A recent study shows that one-third of Sri Lankan workers in the Gulf states had accepted jobs requiring lower status and skills than they had achieved prior to emigration. Other examples of de-skilling include Filipino college graduates working as domestics in the receiving countries. In recent years the creation of new low-skill, low-wage jobs in the United States, alongside a slow increase of job opportunities at higher levels, may have the effect of encouraging this trend.

Another problem concerns the relevance of the skills and experience acquired and the aptitude developed by the migrant workers while abroad. When the industrial structures, technology and work environments diverge widely between sending and receiving countries, the migrants, even if they have enhanced their skills while abroad, may find it difficult to make effective use of them on their return to the home country. Several studies made in the 1980s revealed that these factors contributed to a lack of job opportunities for professionals, even in such middle-income countries as Greece and Turkey, when they returned from Germany. One study among returnees in Pakistan showed that the employers consistently rated the latter higher than workers having no overseas employment. But 81 per cent of the return migrants and 83 per cent of the employers reported that skills acquired by the workers during their overseas employment were not fully used mainly because they were largely irrelevant to the local situation (Azam, 1988).

More frequently, it has been found that even if the returnees acquired relevant and adaptable skills in responsible positions held abroad, they may not be interested to take up a new challenge in the industrial sector of the domestic economy. The most common reasons are inferior or less congenial working conditions or simply a preference for retirement after years of work abroad. A fairly general tendency (for example, in Bangladesh and Pakistan) among those returnees who wish to remain active is to set up businesses of their own. Reluctance to accept low-level jobs, preference for self-employment, a deterioration in the employment situation in the home country – or a combination of these factors – were probably the reasons for a higher level of un-employment among migrants following their return than before emigration, as was revealed by recent surveys in several South Asian countries (e.g. Bangladesh, Pakistan and Sri Lanka).[6] In some cases skilled and enterprising returnees may fail to inject a new impulse for change because of resistance from well-entrenched hierarchies and local jealousies.

However, recent studies in different countries such as Colombia and Mexico[7] as in Greece and Turkey seem to suggest that return migration can be a powerful factor for modernization in small towns and villages. Nigerian migrants returning from Ghana are reported to have intro-duced new crops and contributed to breaking social rigidities that hindered economic change. They may also have contributed to the promotion of joint action in the form of cooperative farming and credit association. In East Africa, studies made in Malawi, Uganda and Zimbabwe provide evidence of emigration and return contributing to construction of modern houses, adoption of improved environmental hygiene and sanitation, acquisition of productive land and establish-ment of small business enterprises (Oucho,1994).

Research has shown that in South Asia (Bangladesh, India, Pakistan and Sri Lanka) returning migrants are highly motivated and full of entrepreneurial drive, even though they may not always succeed in new ventures due to lack of guidance and financial and institutional support. In many cases the return, after having initially created an atmosphere of tension, has led to positive change. But, as with remittances, the benefits of return seem to be generally limited to local areas and communities.

SUMMARY AND CONCLUDING OBSERVATIONS

Differences in the conditions and types of economic migration as well as in the economic and social characteristics of the wide variety of sending countries make it difficult to draw specific conclusions about the impact of these movements, except on a case-by-case basis. Based on the foregoing discussion it is nonetheless possible to present a few general observations on the subject.

Experience confirms that economic migration is no short-cut to development. It will therefore be unwise for the labour-abundant developing countries to regard migration as a panacea for their economic ills. Given favourable conditions, including a conducive policy framework, economic migration can, however, make a significant contribution to development. An optimal policy package for this purpose calls for close collaboration between sending and receiving countries (the role of the latter has not been discussed in this chapter). The challenge before the labour-abundant developing countries is to adopt policies and measures capable of maximizing the benefits of economic migration while minimizing its costs .

As part of such policies the sending-country government needs to be vigilant, without necessarily being too interventionist, in ensuring that the methods of selection and recruitment of migrants are in keeping with its development objectives and that these do not entail abuse and exploitation of migrants. When private agencies operate through a legally constituted enterprise structure, they can facilitate intermediation in the international labour market and export of labour services; it also makes it easier for the government to monitor the movements.

Emigration can provide relief from unemployment in overcrowded areas but its contribution to solving unemployment on a country-wide basis often remains limited, especially when causes of unemployment are of a structural nature. Labour outflows are sometimes associated with greater labour mobility and increased female participation in the labour force. But if there are social and spatial barriers to such mobility, whether lateral or vertical or both, labour and skill shortages can co-exist with unemployment.

In situations where emigrating workers can easily be replaced, the risk of dislocation in production or distortion in the wage structure is limited. Large-scale skill migration can be particularly damaging for a developing economy when skills are scarce and emigrating skills are difficult to replace; it tends to generate a negative multiplier effect both on production and future development of human capital resources.

For many developing countries an effective way of addressing the problem of 'brain drain' lies in strengthening their, hitherto largely neglected, skill- and knowledge-intensive service industries and their increased participation in world trade in such services. Trade-related temporary movement of skilled personnel as service providers can well be a partial substitute for long-term or permanent migration. This is a promising avenue that should be more vigorously pursued, given the opportunities opened up by the General Agreement on Trade in Services.

There is little doubt that remittances enhance the welfare of migrants' families and promote human capital at the household level. They can also provide valuable support to the balance of payments accounts, and help economic development by providing foreign exchange for essential imports. Remittances can ease strains on external accounts following trade liberalization but rarely do they act as the prime determining factor for policy change.

When macro-economic and other conditions are favourable, remittance flows have been found to raise domestic investment. But, essentially, they are a private transfer to the family budget, and should not be confused with, or relied upon as, capital imports. Their investment-creating potential needs to be assessed in the context of the expenditure pattern of non-remittance-receiving household in the same income groups. When the macro-economic effect of remittance expenditure is taken into account its impact on development could be significant. The inflationary effects of remittances are highly sensitive to the elasticity of supply of particular goods and services. Among the main negative consequences of remittances are that the flows are vulnerable to sudden external shocks and that they may delay the process of essential structural adjustment to restore a durable equilibrium in the sending country's external accounts.

Despite some studies showing that migration-related remittances increase income inequality, the available evidence remains inconclusive. In small communities changes in lifestyle and consumption pattern of remittance-receiving families may lead to a feeling of differentiation and weakening of social cohesion.

These and other social effects of emigration are highly culture-specific and can vary widely even within the same country, depending on the socio-economic characteristics of the migrants, nature of social support available to the migrants' families and other local circumstances. Depending on the circumstances, emigration can strengthen family ties and solidarity or increase intra-family problems. Male migration in some cases has meant more responsibilities for women in cultivation, financial management and household decision-making. By contrast, in some other cases it has increased female seclusion and led to a less active role for women left behind. Similarly, the demographic impact is largely influenced by the volume and nature of the outflows, the age and gender composition of the migrants and a complex set of socio-economic variables.

The benefits of return lie mainly in the improvement of human capital of the sending country. But this is dependent on three main conditions. Migrants return home with more productive skills than they would have learned at home; the skills learned abroad are relevant to the home country; the returnees have the willingness and opportunity to use the skills upon return. When these conditions are not fully met, the promises of return migration remain unfulfilled or are only partly realized. In many small communities the return, despite creating some tensions in the initial stage, has led to positive social change and it can be a powerful factor for modernization through the construction of new houses, improvements of roads and other local infrastructures and the setting up of small service establishments. But these benefits are generally confined to local areas and communities.

What, then, should be the overall assessment? In a nutshell, a sending country should be in a position to maximize benefits from emigration when two main sets of conditions are available. First, a flexible economic and social structure; an efficient vocational training system; and financial institutions capable of handling remittances in an honest, effective and imaginative manner. Second, a policy package that fosters and strengthens these conditions and makes the economy better equipped to absorb new ideas and skills and respond positively to external financial stimuli. The benefits of emigration could be significant, but they should not be taken for granted.

NOTES

1   This statement refers to the general trends in contemporary migration literature and its main thrust. Writings of a small group of analysts reveal a noteworthy departure away from these trends but they remain an exception rather than the rule.

2   See ILO/IOM/UNHCR (1994), Geneva. The selection of 98 countries and territories is based on a set of criteria involving stocks of migrants and flows of remittances. The figures possibly are underestimates because of the lack of complete data for emigration and immigration in a number of cases.

3   The export of such labour services is of course only a part of the total economic migration flows.

4   The proposals that have been put forward from time to time to compensate the sending countries for their brain-drain losses include the following: a) repayment by the potential emigrants, prior to their departure, of any education subsidies they have received; (b) introducing a two-tier system of tuition fees under which those paying the higher fees would be free to emigrate and those accepting the subsidy would be required to work in their home country for a fixed number of years; and (c) the payment by the receiving country of the education subsidy or a higher compensation to the country of origin. A detailed review of these and other similar proposals, on which there is already a considerable volume of literature, is outside the scope of this chapter.

5   For a detailed discussion of the subject, see Ghosh, Bimal (forthcoming), *Gains from Global Linkages: Trade in Services and Movements of Natural Persons*, Geneva: International Organization for Migration.

6   See, in this connection, Mahmood, R.A. (1991), 'Bangladesh Return Migrants from the Middle East: Process, Achievement and Adjustment'; Khan, M.F. (1991), 'Migrant Workers to the Arab World: The Experience of Pakistan' and Gunatilleke, G. (1991), 'Sri Lanka', in G. Gunatilleke (ed.) (1991), *Migration to the Arab World. Experience of Returning Migrants, op. cit.*

7   See, for example, Massey, D.R *et al.* (1987), *Return to Aztlan: The Social Process of International Migration from Western Mexico*, Berkeley: University of California Press; and Diaz, L. (1987), *The Impact of Economic Crisis on Rural Migration from Colombia to Venezuela*, Paper submitted at the OECD Seminar on Migration and Development, Paris: OECD.

REFERENCES

Abella, Manolo (1993), 'Role of Formal Labour Schemes in the Development of Third World Countries', *International Migration*, 30 (2/3), p. 398.

Adams R.H. (1991), *The Effects of International Remittances on Poverty, Inequality and Development in Rural Egypt*, Research Report No. 86, Washington DC: International Food Policy Research Institute.

Amin, B.A. and Awny, E.(1985), *International Migration of Egyptian Labour: A Review of the State of the Art* (manuscript report), Ottawa: International Development Research Centre.

Athukorala,P. (1990), 'International Contract Migration and the Reintegration of Return Migrants: The Experience of Sri Lanka', *International Migration Journal*, 24 (2), pp. 323–46.

Azam, Farooq-I (1988), *Monitoring Skill Acquisition, Loss and Utilisation: The Pakistan Pilot Survey*, Bangkok: ILO.

Castillo, M.A. (1994), 'A Preliminary Analysis of Emigration Determinants in Mexico, Central America, Northern South America and the Caribbean', *International Migration*, 32 (2), p. 283.

Choucri, Nazil (1985), '*A Study of Sudanese National Working Abroad*', Cambridge Massachusetts Institute of Technology, Unpublished; quoted in Russell, P. (1992), 'Migration, Remittances and Development', *International Migration*, 30 (3/4), p. 268.

Economist, The, 8 October 1994.

Fernandez, M.A.Z., Alonzo, R.P. and Mendoza, R.E. (1987), *Labour Market Adjustment to Outflows of Skilled Labour: The Philippine Experience*; and *Labour Market Adjustment to Emigration in Pakistan*, Islamabad: ILO.

Ghosh, Bimal (1992), 'Migration, Trade and International Co-operation: Do the Inter-linkages Work?', *International Migration*, 30 (3/4), pp. 378–9.

Ghosh, Bimal (1995), *Movements of People: The Search for a New International Regime*, in *Issues in Global Governance*, The Commission on Global Governance, Kluwer International, London, pp. 405–24.

Ghosh, Bimal (1995), *Gains from Global Linkages: Trade in Services and Movements of Natural Persons*, Geneva: International Organization for Migration (forthcoming).

Glytsos, N. (1990), *Measuring the Income Effects of Migrant Remittances. An Empirical Analysis for Greece*, Athens: Centre for Planning and Economic Research.

Gulati, Leela (1993), *In the Absence of Their Men: The Impact of Male Migration on Women*, New Delhi: Sage Publication.

Gunatilleke, G. (1991), 'Sri Lanka', in G. Gunatilleke (ed.), *Migration to the Arab World: Experience of Returning Migrants*, Tokyo: The United Nations University.

Gunatilleke, G. (1994), *The Economic, Demographic, Socio-cultural and Political Setting for Emigration*, Colombo: Marga Institute, pp. 25–6.

Ibrahim, S. (1982), *The New Arab Social Order: A Study of the Social Impact of Oil*, Boulder, Colorado: Westview Press.

ILO, *International Economic Migration*, November 1993.

ILO/UNDP (1988), *Agenda for Policy: Asian Migration Project*, Bangkok: ILO.

Kamiar, M.S. and Ismail, H. F.(1991), 'Family Ties and Economic Concerns of Migrant Labour Families in Jordan', *International Migration*, 29 (4), pp. 561–72.

Kandil, M. and Metawally, M. F.(1990), 'The Impact of Migrants' Remittances on the Egyptian Economy', *International Migration*, 28 (2) June, pp. 159-80.

Khafagy, F. (1983), 'Socio-economic Impact of Emigration from a Gaza Village', in A. Richards and P.L Martin (eds), *Migration, Mechanisation and Agricultural Labour Markets in Egypt*, Boulder, Colorado: Westview Press

Khafagy, F. (1984*)*, 'Women and Labour Migration: One Village in Egypt', Middle East Research and Information Project, 124, pp. 17–24.

Kim, Sooyong (1983), 'The Labour Migration from Korea to the Middle East: Its Trends and Impacts on the Korean Economy', Paper presented at the Conference on Asian Labour Migration to the Middle East, Honolulu, 1983.

Korale, R.B.M. and Gunapala, G.D.C. (1985*)*, 'Dimensions of Return Migration in Sri Lanka', Paper presented at the Policy Workshop on

International Migration in Asia and the Pacific, Bangkok, 15–21 October 1985.

Mynitti, C. (1984), 'Yemeni Workers Abroad: The Impact on Women', Middle East Research and Information Project, 124, pp. 11–16.

Nishat, Mohammed and Bilgrami, Nighol (1991), 'The Impact of Migrant Workers' Remittances on the Pakistan Economy', *Pakistan Economic and Social Review*, 29 (1), Summer, pp. 21–41.

OECD, SOPEMI, 1993.

Oucho, John O. (1994), *Emigration Dynamics of Eastern African Countries*, Nairobi: Population and Research Institute, University of Nairobi, p. 83.

Roongshivin, P. (1985), 'Survey of the Situation of Thai Returned Migrant Workers for Development of a Re-integration Policy for the Sixth Five Year Plan, 1978–81', Paper presented to the Policy Workshop on International Migration in Asia and the Pacific, Bangkok, 15–21 October 1985.

Rubenstein, H. (1992), 'Migration, Development and Remittances in Rural Mexico', *International Migration*, 30 (2), pp. 127–47.

Seccombe, I.J. and Lawless, R.I.(1988), 'State Intervention and the International Labour Market', in R. Appleyard, (ed.), *The Impact of International Migration on Developing Countries*, Paris: OECD, pp. 69–86.

Shah, Nasra M. (1994), 'An Overview of Present and Future Emigration Dynamics in South Asia', *International Migration*, 32 (2), pp. 217–68.

Smart, John E. (1984), *Worker Circulation Between Asia and the Middle East: The Structural Intersection of Labour Markets*, Paper presented at the Workshop on the Consequences of International Migration, International Union for the Scientific Study of Population, Canberra, 16–19 July 1984.

Taylor, E. (1984), 'Egyptian Migration and Peasant Wives', Middle East Research and Information Project, 124, pp. 3–10.

UNDP (1994), *Human Development Report 1994*, New York and Oxford: Oxford University Press.

UNHCR, *Populations of Concern to UNHCR: A Statistical* Overview, 1993.

United Nations, *World Migrant Population: The Foreign-Born*, 1989.

Utzua, R. (1981), *Population Redistribution Mechanisms as Related to Various Forms of Development in Population Distribution Policies in Development Planning*, New York: United Nations.

Widgren, Jonas (1994), *Multilateral Co-operation to Combat Trafficking in Migrants and the Role of International Organisations*, Vienna: ICPMD. Discussion paper submitted at the IOM Seminar on Trafficking in Migrants, Geneva, 26–28 October 1994.

Zhang Ningxiang, Chu Changyou and Xu Dansong (1992), 'Labour Service Exports from China: Present Situation and Future Potential', quoted in UNCTAD (1993), *Temporary Movement of Persons as Service Providers*, Document TD/B/CN.4/24, p. 9, Geneva.

3 International Migration and Labour Mobility: The Receiving Countries

115 – 58
Global
F22
R23
J61

Vernon M. Briggs, Jr.

Throughout the ascendancy of mankind, migration has been among the most distinguishing behavioural characteristics of the human species. The noted historian William McNeill, in describing the pre-modern experience, has written that 'it is safe to assume that when our ancestors first became fully human they were already migratory' because they were already hunters and, he adds, that 'no dominant species ever spread so far so fast' as have human beings (McNeill, 1987, p. 15). From these early times until the modern era, there was little concern about how migrants might be received wherever they arrived. If the land area was unoccupied, the migrants simply settled it; if it was occupied, the newcomers might be absorbed if they came as individuals but, in numbers, they often had to fight to displace those already there with the outcome of the struggle often being death, enslavement, or exile for the losers. Indeed, much of the recorded history of mankind is a story of repeated invasions of one people by another. Looked at from a long-run perspective, all existing countries are 'nations of immigrants'. It is only a matter of the time frame.

But in a finite spatial world that, in modern times, has been politically demarcated into nation-states and economically organized by industrialization and urbanization pressures, the movement of people and workers was destined to encounter both natural limitations and man-made institutional barriers. Indeed, the confrontation between the urge to migrate by millions of people and the mounting resistance to their efforts in the late 20th century has the likelihood of becoming the 'human crisis of our age' (United Nations Population Fund, 1993, p. 15). For unlike the general experiences of earlier epochs, 'today's migrants are pushing into territory already occupied by others' and 'the recipient areas and countries are already under stress' (United Nations Population Fund, 1993, p. 15).

As of 1992, it is estimated that the available labour force of the world is about 2.5 billion workers. Of this number, about 100 million persons are estimated to be international migrants who are living outside their country of origin (United Nations Population Fund, 1993, p. 7). To the receiving countries, these persons are the sum of the legal immigrants, refugees, asylum seekers, illegal immigrants and non-immigrant workers (i.e., foreign nationals legally permitted to work in the receiving country for a temporary period). Although precise data are unavailable and definitions of residency status differ between nations, it is conservatively estimated that this stock is increasing by about 2 million international migrants a year (Martin, 1994a, p. 179). Due to the prevalence of uncounted illegal immigrants, the actual number is certainly higher. The annual flow is bound to grow throughout the foreseeable future.

While the number of international migrants is substantial, it is important to keep the issue in perspective. The vast preponderance of the world's labour force is not involved. This remains true despite what would seem to be, given the magnitudes of the disparities and the nature of the pressures involved, overpowering reasons for many more to do so. Moreover, only a few nations serve as receiving countries on a regular basis. But it is precisely because there are so few countries that are the destinations of most migrants that the numbers of those who do migrate assume significance and the impact of their presence becomes of consequence.

THE CAUSES OF INCREASING WORLD MIGRATION

Before examining the effects of contemporary migration on receiving nations, it is essential to mention the major forces that are responsible for propelling so many persons into the international migrant streams. They form the context in which the phenomena takes place and, in part, explain the scale and the character of the immigrant flow to which the receiving countries must react.

Paramount among the 'push' factors is the population explosion that is occurring primarily in the less economically developed nations of the world. The world's population of about 5.5 billion people in 1993 is growing by about 98 million persons a year. Of this number, 93 per cent of the growth in 1990 occurred in the less developed nations of the world and it is projected to be 95 per cent by 2000 (United Nations Populations Fund, 1993, p. 1).

The world's population is also rapidly urbanizing. By the beginning of the 21st century, it is estimated that over half the world's population will live in cities. In the 1990s, 83 per cent of the growth in the world's population is projected to occur in cities. One-third of the world's urban population currently live in cities of more than one million people. The movement from rural to urban population centres is a characteristic of virtually all national economies. But the shift is most acute, in terms of the numbers of people involved, in the less developed nations where their 'cities' capacity to provide economic opportunities and even modest levels of support services to newcomers is declining rather than increasing' (United Nations Population Fund, 1993 p. 5).

There is also the issue of refugee movements. In 1991 the United Nations estimated that there were 17 million refugees outside of their native countries in the world with 87 per cent of them being located in less developed nations (United Nations Population Fund, 1993, p. 7). The instability of the governments in many less developed nations is frequently cited as the cause of these refugee outflows. The instability is caused as much by social and economic conditions as it is by political factors. Sometimes the ensuing violence is the result of ethnic and religious differences between factions within countries. But more often than not, the root cause of the political instability stems from the soaring population growth rate in these countries that serves as a persistently negative influence on any efforts to achieve sustainable economic growth and development. The growth in population is directly linked to the inability of governments to provide adequate health, housing and education. It also instigates conflicts over land use and ownership. Without population controls, emigration becomes an ever-appealing option.

Last, of course, there is the fact that migration pressures are spawned by the mounting economic inequities between those who live in 'have' countries and those who live in 'have-not' countries. Between 1950 and 1993, 'per capita income in the rich countries has almost tripled while in the poorer countries there has been no improvement' (United Nations Population Fund, 1993, p. 8). Enhanced communication systems in the world now enable those in poorer countries to see what they do not have and improved transportation systems now provide the means by which many persons in these countries may actually avail themselves of opportunities for a better life. Once the process begins, information networks quickly develop among families and friends, which seek to perpetuate and expand the movements if the chances to do so are available.

While international migration cannot possibly resolve the dilemmas posed by the magnitude of these aforementioned pressures, it is viewed by many individuals as a remedy to their specific plight. But such migration can only occur if there is a place to go.

THE THEORETICAL EFFECTS OF IMMIGRATION ON RECEIVING NATIONS

If standard economic theory of labour market operations (i.e., neoclassical economic theory) is applied to the analysis of the migration process, the effects of immigration on receiving nations are the same as any other exogenous increase in the supply of labour. If unrestricted by governmental policies, the operation of supply-and-demand forces will lead to the establishment of an equilibrium position between the sending and receiving nations. Those countries with a slow rate of economic growth and a surplus of labour will witness out-migration to those countries with higher economic growth rates and labour shortages. A self-adjusting process will occur. Spatial differences between the demand for and the supply of labour will automatically be reconciled between the sending and the receiving nations. Any efforts by a receiving nation to protect its labour force from the competitive effects of immigration are viewed as self-defeating. For in the absence of market forces to reduce wages and to lower work standards (i.e., costs), businesses will invest in capital-intensive rather than labour intensive forms of technology in order to compete in an increasingly internationally competitive market place. Restrictions on immigration, therefore, would cause unemployment in any country that sought to impose them. They would cause inefficiency. Trade union or government policies that seek to protect prevailing wages, employment standards and working conditions by restricting immigration would, in turn, be blamed for the ensuing unemployment that is the result of their actions which inhibit what would otherwise be a self-equilibrating adjusting process that, theoretically, provides full employment.

Conceptually, the arguments used to support free trade between nations (by eliminating tariffs and quotas on imports and government subsidies on exports) are identical to those that provide the theoretical rationale for the unimpeded movement of labour between nations (by eliminating immigration and emigration restrictions on the entry and exit of labour). Ultimately, the application of this theoretical paradigm can only be that wage rates in high-wage countries (e.g., the advanced industrial democracies) are reduced and in low-wage countries (e.g., Third World nations) they are raised. The same can be said for other labour and employment standards (i.e., occupational health, safety, child labour, wage and working hours laws) that exist between nations. There will be pressures towards equalization which means lower labour standards in the industrial democracies but, theoretically, improvement in employment conditions in the less developed world.

One advocate in the United States for the pursuit of free movement of international labour is the editorial staff of *The Wall Street Journal*. In a widely cited editorial in 1988 that was critical of US governmental efforts to legislate against illegal immigration, it stated 'if Washington still wants to do something about immigration, we propose a five word Constitutional Amendment: There shall be open borders' (*The Wall Street Journal*, 1989, p. 6). Julian Simon, who is associated with the libertarian-oriented Cato Institute, is also an outspoken advocate of the pursuit of an open-door policy (Simon, 1991).

Ironically, it has been various members of the Department of Economics at the University of Chicago over the years – who are otherwise known as the champions of the pursuit of free market economic policies – who have spoken out most forcefully against the neoclassical position calling for no restrictions by receiving countries on the international movement of labour. Henry Simons, one of the intellectual founders of the 'Chicago School', bluntly stated that:

> Wholly free immigration, however, is neither attainable or desirable. To insist that a free trade program is logically or practically incomplete without free migration is either disingenuous or stupid. Free trade may and should raise living standards everywhere .... Free immigration would level standards, perhaps without raising them anywhere. (Simons, 1948, p. 251)

It is Henry Simons's recommendation, therefore, that 'as regards immigration policy, the less said the better' (Simons, 1984, p. 251). Milton Friedman, Simons's intellectual heir at Chicago, has taken Simons's advice to heart. Although known to share Simons's views on the topic, Friedman completely ignored immigration policy in his famous book, *Capitalism and Freedom*, in which he outlines the role of government policy in a market-oriented society (Friedman, 1962). The same can be said for his treatment of immigration in his subsequent best seller, *Free to Choose*. In it, only a few positive anecdotes are made about the adjustment experiences of a few immigrants at the turn of the 20th century but the overall impact of immigration policy on the US economy is ignored (Friedman and Friedman, 1990). Much of the advancement in real wages and expanded job opportunities that Friedman attributes to the free market economic system for US workers in general and black workers in particular over the middle decades of the 20th century took place during the years when the US had highly restrictive immigration policies in place and immigration levels were rapidly declining. But the beneficial labour market outcomes of these governmental interventions to restrict immigration are simply ignored. It is also bewildering that the praise Friedman heaps upon Margaret Thatcher for the free market policies she championed as Prime Minister of Great Britain during the 1980s does not mention the highly restrictive immigration policies she put in place during her tenure. To this day, Britain's immigration policies remain the most restrictive in Western Europe (Martin, 1994b; and Coleman, 1994).

Likewise, Melvin Reder – also of the Chicago economics' faculty – has pointed out that 'free immigration would cause a rapid equalization of per capita income across countries accomplished primarily by leveling downward the income of the more affluent' and, for this reason, he concluded 'I resist this proposal' (Reder, 1982, p.

31). Earlier Reder had written in 1963 – before mass immigration to the United States resumed later in that same decade – that 'a great flow of immigration will injure labour market competitors with immigrants; these are, predominately Negroes, Puerto Ricans, unskilled immigrants presently able to enter the country, and native rural–urban migrants (Negro and White)' (Reder, 1963, p. 227). He also noted that the employment and income opportunities of 'married women, youth, and aged persons' would be adversely affected by substantial increases in immigration (Reder, 1963, pp. 227–9). Reder also points out that the United States and other 'Western democracies' had, prior to the 1960s, made substantial progress towards improving the inequalities in income distribution within these nations as the result of 'deliberate state action' to restrict immigration over the prior 50 years' (Reder, 1963, p. 230). Thus, there are significant equity issues that arise for receiving nations when mass immigration occurs.

On the day that it was announced that Gary Becker, another member of the Chicago economics' faculty, had won the 1992 Nobel Memorial Prize in Economics, he published a commentary in *The Wall Street Journal* that explained why restrictive immigration policies were essential for the contemporary United States experience and for the other industrialized democracies which are would-be destinations for millions of immigrants from the Third World. He contrasted the economic setting of the large-scale immigration experience of the United States at the beginning of the 20th century with the economic setting at the end of the century. He observed:

> But the world is now a very different place. Because of the expanded welfare state, immigration is no longer a practical policy. These days open immigration would merely induce people in poorer countries to emigrate to the United States and other developed countries to collect generous transfer payments. (Becker, 1992, p. A–14)

Hence, there are historical realities associated with the differential development of social policies between nations which may be affected by immigration.

Given these views, it is not surprising that the role of immigration as a potential influence on the supply of labour to would-be receiving nations is one of the least examined features of contemporary economic analysis. The leading advocates of the neoclassical paradigm of labour market operations have essentially agreed to say as little as possible on the subject. This posture clearly reflects a normative judgement on their part that such equilibrating adjustments are not in the national interests of these receiving nations despite the alleged benefits that this model usually propounds for those who adopt its non-interventionist principles. In other words, immigration is a time-sensitive topic. Its merits depend on past historical events as well as present circumstances – not theoretical dogma. As the renowned scholar of the history of economic analysis, Joseph Schumpeter, has stated, unless the examination of a particular economic issue 'presents a minimum of historical aspects, no amount of correctness, originality, rigor, or elegance will prevent a sense of lacking direction and meaning' to what is being examined (Schumpeter, 1954, p. 4). Such is certainly the case with the study of immigration.

Thus, the neoclassical model, the bulwark of free market economic analysis, has an Achilles' Heel. It is immigration. Even the strongest intellectual advocates of the application of free market economics have made immigration the exception to the belief that the neoclassical model should be the universal paradigm for the design of national and international economic policies. For in this realm of economic concerns, even neoclassicists seem willing to concede that support for international labour migration is a relative concept.

The efficacy of international labour immigration, therefore, depends upon a pragmatic assessment of both the institutional arrangements and the prevailing economic circumstances in the receiving countries at a given time. Some times, immigration may be a desirable public policy option; other times it may not be. The unrestricted movement of international labour, therefore, is not a universal principle to be pursued simply for the sake of seeking enhanced efficiency in the worldwide labour market. There are other factors associated with perceived national interests to be considered which may be far more consequential to receiving nations than any theoretical or real loss in labour utilization that might result as a consequence of restricting international labour mobility. As Reder has eloquently written, 'immigration policy inevitably reflects a kind of national selfishness of which the major beneficiaries are the least fortunate among us. We could not completely abandon this policy even if we desired to do so' (Reder, 1963, p. 230).

THE RECEIVING COUNTRIES AND THE CIRCUMSTANCES UNDER WHICH IMMIGRANTS ARE ADMITTED

Aside from the political asylum issue (which is a special case that disproportionately affects entry into neighbouring nations to any country beset by political turmoil), there are essentially three geographic clusters of nations that, from a numerical standpoint, currently receive most of the world's immigrants (see Table 3.1). Each reflects a particular set of historical circumstances and institutional arrangements that have shaped their individual attitudes. There is no overarching pattern to explain why a few countries permit significant numbers of workers from other countries to enter their countries while the vast preponderance of nations in the world do not. Each case is, therefore, time sensitive. As conditions change, so does the degree of receptivity of these receiving nations. There are no universal principles involved.

The North America Case

As Philip Martin has noted 'the United States and Canada [currently] ... accept about 1 million immigrants annually, or about 90 per cent of all the immigrants that the industrial democracies plan to accept' in the early 1990s (Martin, 1994a, p. 180). Both countries also experience significant additional inflows of illegal immigration which they have sought to combat but not with much success. Each, however, has taken an entirely different policy approach to immigrant admissions.

In the case of the United States, immigration played a major role in the pre-industrialization era of the emergence of the nation as an economic superpower (Briggs, 1984, Chapters 2 and 3; and Briggs, 1992, Chapters 3–6). Following the end of its colonial era in 1776, the new nation expanded geographically across the North American continent to embrace a vast land area that contained an enormous amount of natural resources, rich soil, large quantities of fresh water, and a temperate climate but relatively few people (the small indigenous population which resisted incorporation has never been included in the economic development of the nation).

Table 3.1 Gross inflows of foreign population to selected countries, 1985–1990 (thousands)

Country	1985	1986	1987	1988	1989	1990
Europe						
Belgium	37.5	39.3	40.1	38.2	43.5	52.3
France[a]	43.4	38.3	39.0	44.0	53.2	63.1
Germany	324.4	378.6	414.9	545.4	649.5	NA
Netherlands	40.6	46.9	47.4	50.8	51.5	60.1
Norway[b]	14.9	16.5	15.2	16.4	14.0	11.7
Sweden[c]	13.4	19.4	19.0	24.9	28.9	23.9
Switzerland[d]	59.4	66.8	71.5	76.1	80.4	101.4
United Kingdom[e]	55.4	47.8	46.0	49.3	49.7	52.4
North America						
Canada[f]	84.3	99.2	152.1	161.9	192.0	213.6
United States[f]	570.0	601.7	601.5	643.0	1,090.9	1,536.5

Notes:

a   Includes holders of provisional work permits and foreigners admitted on family reunification grounds. Does not include residents of EEC countries who have not been brought in by the International Migration Office.
b   Entries of foreigners intending to stay longer than six months.
c   Some short duration entries are not counted.
d   Entries of foreigners with annual permits and those with permanent permits who return after a temporary stay abroad. Seasonal and frontier workers are excluded.
e   Entries correspond to permanent settlers within the meaning of the 1971 Immigration Act and subsequent amendments.
f   Permanent settlers only.

Source: Système d'Observation Permanente des Migration (SOPEMI) of the Organization for Economic Cooperation and Development (Paris), 1992. Asylum seekers excluded.

[Note: This table is taken from Beth J. Asch, *Emigration and Its Effects on the Sending Countries* (Santa Monica: RAND, 1994) Table 1.1, p. 4 and reprinted with permission from RAND.]

Created as an independent nation at exactly the same time that the Industrial Revolution occurred in England and in parts of Continental Europe, the United States was 'born running' with these new technological developments. But it needed a vast urban labour force to capitalize on the productive capabilities of machine technology. To cut a long story short, immigrants in the 19th and early 20th centuries became the source of the needed urban labour supply during these crucial formative years of the US economy. As Stanley Lebergott has observed in his epic study of the development of the US labour force, 'somewhat surprisingly, the greatest beneficiaries of the flow of immigrant labour [in the 19th century] was never agriculture though farming was our primary industry' (Lebergott, 1964, p. 28). Rather, it was the urban economy in general and the manufacturing, mining, construction and transportation industries in particular that expanded by their presence. But when the frontiers of the country were overcome at the turn of the 20th century, it was not long before immigration was sharply restricted – beginning in 1914. In part the restrictions reflected legitimate economic concerns that the mass immigration of the previous three decades had depressed wages, hampered unionization, and caused unemployment; in part they also reflected nativist social reactions to the ethnic, racial and religious diversity that the mass immigration of that era also brought (Briggs, 1984, pp. 31–54). For almost the next 60 years, the significance of immigration rapidly receded and the expansion of the economy turned to the incorporation of domestic labour reserves – most specifically those in the nation's vast rural areas where workers were being displaced by this time by the rapid mechanization of agriculture that had begun in earnest in the 1880s. One of the major beneficiaries of the cessation of mass immigration was the nation's black population who, since being freed from slavery in 1865, were still concentrated in the rural South. It was not until mass immigration ended in 1914 that 'the Great Migration' of blacks to the North and the West could commence (Briggs, 1992, pp. 51–2).

Indicative of the declining significance of immigration on American life following the restrictions imposed in the 1920s is the fact that the percentage of the US population that was foreign born consistently fell from 13.2 per cent in 1920 to 4.7 per cent in 1970. During this period from 1920 to 1970, the US economy sustained the greatest increases in real wages, employment levels and production output in its entire economic history. It was also the time period when the nation adopted an extensive array of progressive social policies pertaining to employment standards, collective bargaining and civil rights (Briggs, 1995).

It was not until the mid-1960s that the mass immigration phenomenon was accidentally revived as a result of domestic political events and immigration once again became a significant feature of the US economy (Briggs, 1992, Chapters 5 and 6). A new admission system was put into place in 1965 which provided that family reunification would be the primary criterion for the admission of legal immigrants. This change inadvertently opened the door of immigration priority to persons of the Western Hemisphere (from Mexico and various Caribbean countries in particular) who had not been covered by the earlier legislative efforts to restrict Eastern Hemisphere immigration and who, by the 1960s, had established significant immigrant communities in selected urban areas of the US Originally family admissions were allocated 74 per cent of all available visas. In 1980, when refugee admissions were separated from the legal admission categories, the percentage of visas for family members rose to 80 per cent. It is also important to note that many of the refugees who have been admitted during the post-1965 era were able to use their admission as an opportunity to secure the subsequent admission of their extended family members. In 1990, a new category of 'diversity immigrants' was added to the nation's immigration system. It is supposed to correct the inadvertent result caused by the adoption of the family admission system in 1965 which greatly favoured immigration from Asia and Latin America (during the 1980s, about 85 per cent of immigrants to the United States came from these two regions). The diversity admission category is supposed to increase the flow of immigrants from the traditional pre-1965 source countries in Europe and Africa. With the Immigration Act of 1990, therefore, the percentage of admission visas allocated on criteria other than actual labour market needs remained at 80 per cent (it will be 79 per cent beginning in 1995). Thus, only about 20 per cent of the available visas (i.e., 140,000 visas) each year are allocated on the basis of actual labour market needs (and even this figure overstates the actual number admitted for this economic purpose since all accompanying family members – spouses and children – of employment-based immigrants are counted as part of the 140,000 visas). Thus, the legal admission system which, since 1990, provides for the annual admission of 700,000 immigrants a year (it declines to 675,000 immigrants beginning in 1995) is designed primarily to serve political goals despite the fact that annual immigrant flows of this aggregate magnitude have significant economic implications. It is also important to note when considering the overall effect of immigration on the US labour market and economy to remember that the figures do not include the annual admission of about 130,000 refugees; 10,000 asylum seekers (with a backlog of about 300,000 asylum applicants pending in mid-1994); about 450,000 non-immigrant workers permitted to work legally in the US each year; or an estimated 300,000 illegal immigrants who enter each year (to join about 4 million illegal immigrants already in the country). It is also the case that the United States granted an amnesty to about 3 million former illegal aliens in 1986 which permitted them to begin the process of legally adjusting their status over the following several years. As a result, it is estimated that over 10 million immigrants entered the United States in the 1980s which made it the highest number of immigrants admitted in any single decade in the country's history. By 1990, the foreign born officially accounted for 7.9 per cent of the population (with the real rate undoubtedly higher due to uncounted illegal immigrants). Moreover, in 1991, over 1.8 million persons entered the country or adjusted their status to become permanent resident aliens – the highest number of immigrants to do so in any single year in the country's history. Hence, the decade of the 1990s should set yet a new record for immigrant admissions. It is not surprising, therefore, that an international social science research team observed in its comprehensive study of American life that 'America's biggest import is people' and concluded that 'at a time when attention is directed to the general decline in American exceptionalism, American immigration continues to flow at a rate unknown elsewhere in the world' (Oxford Analytica, 1986, p. 20).

In addition to the United States, Canada has been a net receiver of immigrants for permanent settlement every year since 1950. In the process, its population has doubled and, by 1990, its foreign-born residents had soared to 16.2 per cent of the country's population. The post-World War II decision to open Canada to immigration was prompted by the nation's business sector in response to a perceived labour shortage. The admission system that has evolved contrasts sharply with that of the United States. Specifically, 'economic issues have been far more important to Canadians than to Americans' (Reimers and Troper, 1992, p. 15). Consequently, the Canadian system does not have a fixed annual ceiling but rather one that allows the number to be admitted to be annually determined by administrative decisions. The three admission categories – family reunification, economic and humanitarian – can also be adjusted annually to respond to evolving circumstances. In practice, family reunification has been used far less in Canada than in the United States (in 1989, for example, only 32 per cent of the admitted immigrants came under family reunification provisions while 49 per cent were admitted on the basis of actual employment needs of business) with the remainder being admitted on humanitarian grounds (Center for Immigration Studies, 1992, p. C–4). A point system that rewards human capital attributes and labour market needs is used to determine those who are admitted for economic purposes. Although the annual number of admissions fluctuates, it has been tending to rise in recent years (from 84,000 in 1985 to almost 250,000 in 1992). In late 1994, however, Canada announced that it was sharply reducing its ceiling to between 190,000 and 215,000 immigrants a year in 1995 (Clayton, 1994, p. 6). It also announced it was reducing the percentage to be admitted on the basis of family ties and increasing the percentage for those admitted on the basis of employment needs.

Western Europe

It has been estimated that 'some 15 million people entered Western Europe as migrants between 1980 and 1992' (United Nations Population Fund, 1993, p. 16). They have joined an almost equal number of foreign-born persons already living in these countries. Germany has been the principal recipient. By 1990 its foreign resident population was 5.2 million people (or 8.4 per cent of the population – a figure that does not include foreign-born persons who have already been naturalized). The second largest receiver of immigrants has been France. In 1990, 'foreign residents' made up 6.4 per cent of the French population while there were more than one million additional foreign-born persons who had already acquired citizenship and another half million French citizens living in the country who were born in the various French overseas territories and departments.

For much of the 19th and early 20th centuries, Western Europe was an area of emigration. But with the events associated with World War II, this pattern unexpectedly changed. The story has been extensively told elsewhere (Castles, 1989; Bohning, 1984; Rist, 1978; and Cross, 1983). In brief, the physical rebuilding of Western Europe in the aftermath of the extensive destruction of the war led to an increase in the demand for labour. The enormous loss of human life during the war, however, meant that the supply of labour in these countries was unable to respond in the short run. Chronic labour shortages developed and inflationary wage pressures were triggered. As a result, most Western European countries entered into a programme of importing non-immigrant workers under contractual agreements from the less developed regions around the Mediterranean Basin. There was never any intention that these 'temporary workers' would remain or that they would bring their families with them for settlement purposes. The workers were supposed to be regularly rotated so that they would not become attached to the Western European labour market. Typically, the rotation did not occur. When the Arab oil boycott of 1973–74 caused both prices and unemployment to soar in Western Europe, the reaction was to cause these countries to abandon (or greatly reduce) their reliance on the use of non-immigrant labour. But starting such a labour importation programme proved to be much easier than stopping it (Miller and Martin, 1982). By 1973, many of the so-called 'guestworkers' had established deep roots in the receiving countries and many indicated they would not leave voluntarily. In fact, the foreign-born population has continued to grow since 1973 because most European nations have permitted subsequent family reunification to take place; illegal immigration has flourished; and a large wave of asylum-seekers have fled the political turmoil of this era in Eastern Europe, the Near East and Northern Africa.

In response to the unanticipated growth in the foreign-born population and in conjunction with the coterminous formation of the European Economic Community (which since November 1993 is known as the European Union or EU), Western European countries have moved to create uniform as well as restrictive immigration and refugee policies for persons from non-member nations while simultaneously easing restrictions on the movement of people and workers between EU member nations (van de Kaa, 1993). Germany and France, in particular, have taken steps in the early 1990s to significantly restrict immigrant inflows. In July 1993, Germany overhauled its hitherto liberal political asylum policies in favor of a much more restrictive policy and France announced in 1993 a new 'zero-net immigration policy' (Kinzer, 1991, p. A-1; Darnton, 1993, p. A-1; *The Economist*, 1993, p. 57; Waldman, 1993, p. A-6; and Riding, 1993, p. A-8). Most other Western Europe countries have also taken steps to tighten their policies pertaining to illegal immigration and to limit political asylum eligibility.

The Oil-Producing Nations of the Near East and North Africa

Several of the oil-producing countries of the Near East have, collectively, become major receivers of non-immigrant workers for work in their petroleum and construction industries as well as to perform household service. These countries have small native-born populations but, because of the accumulation of wealth derived from their oil exports, they have had difficulty finding native-born workers willing to fill jobs that require physical effort or that are of a menial nature. It is estimated that 45 per cent of the non-immigrant workers in the region are employed in Saudi Arabia (Asch, 1994, pp. 4–5). Libya, the United Arab Emirates and Iraq are also major recipients of such foreign workers from Third World nations. It is estimated that non-immigrant workers account for as much as 36 per cent of the labour force in Saudi Arabia and 55 per cent in Libya (United Nations Population Fund, 1993, p. 17). There is little prospect that many of these workers will have the opportunity to remain permanently in these countries nor are they free to work in occupations or industries other than those to which they have been contracted.

Other Receiving Nations

There are several other receiver countries that deserve brief mention even though the scale of the respective flows into these countries is small when compared to the situations in the primary receiver countries. In some instances, their experiences are similar to those of the major receivers but in others they differ significantly.

Australia is a country that significantly revised its immigration policy in 1958 away from its restrictive past (with respect to whom and how many immigrants it would admit). In the 1970s, the government initiated an 'active' immigration policy. In 1970–71, immigration reached a record high for a single year of 174,000 immigration admissions. Like Canada, Australia has an administrative policy that allows the level of immigration to vary annually as determined by national priorities. Annual immigration ceilings in the 1980s were about 120,000 a year but by 1992 the figure had fallen to 80,000. The numerical importance of immigration to Australia can be gauged from the fact that in 1987 the foreign-born population accounted for over 21 per cent of its population.

For many years after its immigration policy was revised in 1958, the basis for admission was primarily economic. It was designed essentially to meet specific labour market needs. But by late 1975 the political decision to raise immigration levels was matched by decisions to change the selection criteria. Family reunification emerged as the first priority. The decisions were the products of domestic political factors associated with efforts 'to appease' ethnic minorities (both Southern Europeans and Asians) (Birrell, 1984, p. 66). In 1992, over 55 per cent of the available visas were allocated to family migrants. Most of the remainder were reserved for skilled immigrants (38 per cent) whose entry eligibility is determined on a point system that rewards human capital attributes (Center for Immigration Studies, 1992, p. A-4). Humanitarian admissions and a small 'special eligibility' group make up the balance.

Israel has been a significant receiver of immigrants since it became an independent state in 1948 (Center for Immigration Studies, undated). Immigration, however, plays such a unique role in Israel that its role as a receiver is mentioned only for the sake of completeness of coverage. At the time of its inception, Israel found itself being a small land area surrounded by Arab nations hostile to its existence. It also had a significant Arab (i.e., Palestinian) population living within its borders. Hence, its pro-immigration policy has been based firmly on national security considerations. It also has unique religious overtones. The country was created on the principle that it sought to 'regather' the descendants of the lost tribes of biblical times. The Law of Return of 1950 guarantees people of the Jewish faith throughout the world the right to immigrate. There are, therefore, no numerical limits on Jewish immigration. Over 2.2 million immigrants have entered Israel since 1948 with 418,000 entering between 1989 and 1992. The surge in immigration since 1989 has been the consequence of the breakup of the former Soviet Union – Soviet *émigrés* accounting for 88 per cent of post-1989 arrivals. Unemployment in Israel has been high during this recent period and there is extensive evidence of underemployment in its labour force as many of the recent immigrants have been highly educated, skilled and talented. Nonetheless, labour force considerations play no appreciable role in immigration decisions by the government. It also has very liberal social welfare programmes for its populace. The lack of attention of its immigration policies to economic factors, however, does have its domestic critics (Marcus, 1994, p. A-1). As for non-Jews, they may immigrate but relatively few (less than 20 per cent) of those who apply are admitted.

Japan, of course, has been the exception to the rule in the post-World War II era with regard to its policies on immigration. It too was devastated by the war and it also suffered a shortage of labour as the result of extensive casualties. But, in sharp contrast to the experience of Western European countries, it conscientiously avoided the immigrant option. Instead it followed a reconstruction policy based on capital-intensive investments that substituted automatic machines for labour and an active human resource development strategy designed to enhance upward job mobility for its work force through educational attainment and skill acquisition. In the process, Japan has emerged as the only large advanced industrial economy in Asia and it has consistently had low unemployment rates.

Despite tight labour market conditions, Japan has shown no interest in supplementing its labour force through the use of immigration for the purpose of permanent settlement. It is the only industrialized democracy to consistently adhere to 'a zero immigration policy' (Brimelow, 1993, pp. 44–5). It is even reported that official 'Japanese entry statistics don't seem to recognize the concept of an immigrant as opposed to a visitor' (Brimelow, 1993, p. 44). The tight labour market of the mid-1980s, however, has led to limited use of non-immigrant workers (despite government actions to reduce the incidence of their usage) and to a mounting problem of illegal immigration due to visa 'overstayers' from other Asian nations (United Nations Population Fund, 1993 p. 19; Sterngold, 1989, p. A-6; and Morita and Sassen, 1994).

There are also other Asian countries that do not formally encourage immigration but which have experienced significant economic growth which are also turning to the use of non-immigrant workers and are experiencing growing problems with illegal immigration due to visa 'overstayers'. Among these countries are Taiwan and Singapore. It is also reported that the issue of allowing non-immigrant workers to be employed in Korea has been the subject of 'major debate' within government circles and with the business sector in 1994 (United Nations Population Fund, 1993, p. 19).

In Africa, there is also regional migration. As of the early 1990s, Libya, the Ivory Coast, Nigeria and South Africa have been the significant receiving countries. The extensive use of contract workers in Libya has already been discussed. In terms of percentage of its population, the Ivory Coast has the largest number of foreign-born residents (30 per cent) in 1990 (United Nations Population Fund, 1993, p. 19). Most of its immigrants are believed to be illegal entrants. The same can be said for Nigeria. As for South Africa, a substantial portion of its foreign-born population are also believed to be illegal immigrants although the country has made substantial use of non-immigrant foreign workers for unskilled jobs in certain industries.

THE EFFECTS ON THE RECEIVING NATIONS

While most countries permit foreigners to visit, there is no legal obligation nor is there any international human right that requires such countries to allow foreigners to reside or to work within their borders. There is usually a perceived national interest objective at a particular time that explains those decisions to do so. Enabling legislation is required that sets forth the explicit intentions of the receiving nation. But politics being what it is – 'the art of compromise'– the legislative mandates often include multiple objectives (e.g., to reunify families; to settle unoccupied land; to meet labour shortages; to accomplish humanitarian goals; to meet foreign policy objectives; or to accommodate special interest groups). Moreover, despite the best of intentions in drafting immigration legislation, experience has vividly demonstrated that there are often unintended consequences associated with whatever is ultimately enacted. Hence, rather than attempt to evaluate such complex policies on the basis of their expressed objectives, it is preferable to examine the effects of immigration in the light of the three issues raised earlier: efficiency, equity and social policy development.

Efficiency

The clearest rationale for the promotion of labour mobility through the use of immigration is to increase efficiency in labour markets. As noted earlier, immigration can be used as a way to reduce costs. But even members of the 'Chicago School' have resisted such an explicit rationale for the use of such policies. Indeed, the Immigration and Nationality Act of 1952 specifically forbids the entry of non-family-related immigrants (refugees are not covered) into the United States if qualified citizens are available, able and willing to do the work or if their presence will adversely affect prevailing wages and/or working conditions.(U.S. Codes, Volume 8, p. 1182). Thus, the US Secretary of Labor must certify that such results will not occur before any employment-based immigrants may enter (Briggs, 1984, pp. 70–71). No receiving country is willing to explicitly endorse the notion that immigration policy should be used to reduce wages or to worsen prevailing working conditions.

But the United States and Canada – the principal receiving countries for planned immigration – are willing to use immigration as a means of filling existing job vacancies and of forestalling potential increases in wages or improvements in working conditions for certain categories of workers which might otherwise occur under conditions of full employment. Thus, they are willing to admit skilled workers whose ranks are not easy to increase in the short run and whose numbers are costly to increase (because they require human capital expenditures in order to be prepared for such jobs) in the long run. In a sense, this is a way to 'brain drain' the sending countries of their 'best and their brightest' talents which may have serious overtones for the welfare of these sending countries over the long haul.

It is worth noting, as a corollary, that both the United States and Canada have recognized that they should not use immigration policy in contemporary times as a means of recruiting unskilled workers who are not family related to citizens. Canada uses its point system to screen out most such unskilled workers while the United States has a specified legislative mandate since 1990 that no more than 10,000 employment-based visas a year can be granted to unskilled workers.

Despite charges of 'elitism' from immigrant advocate groups, the rationale for restricting the entry of such unskilled workers is clear. Unlike skilled work, anyone can do unskilled work by definition (Briggs, 1993). Hence, there is no reason for any advanced industrial nation to use immigration as a means of attracting unskilled workers for permanent settlement unless the country is at full employment. Skilled workers who are unemployed may not like to do unskilled work, but they can do it. The reverse, however, is not true. Unskilled workers cannot fill skilled jobs when such jobs are vacant. Hence, the welfare of unskilled citizen workers, as Reder noted, requires governmental protection from immigrants.

The use of immigration policy to meet specific employment needs, however, is only one aspect of the immigration systems of countries like the United States and Canada. Hence, the actual labour market consequences of the immigration policies of these countries can be quite different from the aforementioned efforts that nominally seek to protect the domestic labour force from adverse economic competition. As all immigrants must ultimately work to support themselves and their families (or to be supported by those who do), the ultimate concern is what is the effect of all immigrants on labour markets regardless of what legal admission criterion or illegal mode that they actually enter under.

As the criteria for admission of most immigrants (i.e., those who enter as family members, diversity immigrants or as refugees) to the United States has nothing to do with their human capital endowments nor whether there is any need for persons with their skills, talents, or educational achievements, or whether they are needed in the geographic locations where they settle, it is not surprising that the mounting tide of research has found a labour market mismatch. Despite the fact that some immigrants of the post-1965 era do meet the needs of the rapidly changing US labour market, it is mostly accidental that they do. The vast majority do not. Specific studies of the foreign-born population have found that the immigrants of the post-1965 era have less schooling, lower earnings, lower labour force participation rates, higher incidence of poverty and higher unemployment rates than earlier waves of immigrants at similar stages of entry (Borjas, 1990; Borjas, Freeman and Katz, 1992; Meisenheimer, 1992; and Chiswick, 1986). Labour market studies also show that immigrants are disproportionately concentrated in occupations and industries that are in decline and are located in the central cities of urban areas in six major states (California, New York, Texas, Florida, New Jersey and Illinois) where unemployment is generally higher than it is in the state in which they live and of the nation as a whole (Briggs, 1992, Chapters 7 and 8). Given the fact that US immigration policy is essentially designed to meet political objectives, it is not surprising that it fails to be consistent with the nation's evolving economic needs and, in fact, is substantially at odds with those needs. The 1990 Census disclosed, for instance, that 25 per cent of all foreign-born adults (25 years and older) had less than a 9th grade education (compared to only 10 per cent of native-born adults). It also showed that only 58 per cent of the foreign born had a high school degree (whereas 77 per cent of the native born did). Collectively, US immigration policy is supplying a disproportionate number of poorly educated, unskilled, non-English-speaking immigrants into local labour markets at the very time when increasing numbers of such workers are not needed. Already having a substantial number of unskilled citizen workers (e.g., the US Department of Education estimates that half the adult population – or 90 million people – were not proficient in reading or arithmetic in 1992), it is impossible to justify adding to their numbers by immigration at this juncture in the nation's economic development. By no stretch of the imagination can such policy indifference be said to be an efficient way to expand the nation's labour supply in a service dominated, increasingly technologically-oriented and internationally-competitive labour market.

As for Canada, the fact that a point system that rewards human capital factors is used as the primary entry device would seem to lessen the probability of there being a mismatch between the immigrant flow and the needs of its labour market. But, as noted earlier, immigration levels were rising in Canada prior to the announced reductions in late 1994. This meant that other criteria not related to actual labour market needs were dominant in the early 1990s. But with unemployment increasing into double digit figures in the 1990s, the Canadian immigration system could not indefinitely adhere to a politically dominated policy that manifested little concern about possible incongruities with the nation's economic trends. In late 1994, it seems, Canada has decided to confront reality.

In the case of Australia, the traditional use of labour market criteria to govern entry gave way during the 1980s to the more politically popular family reunification goals as the principal rationale for its immigration policy. But the increases in unemployment in the country in the 1990s have been matched by significant decreases in the annual levels of immigration which implies that economic considerations were not entirely abandoned in the administration of its immigration policy.

As for Western Europe and the Near East, it does not make any sense to try to assess their prevailing policies on efficiency grounds. In the case of Western Europe, family reunification, refugee accommodation and illegal immigration do not provide a means of assuring that immigrants are being admitted on the basis of labour market needs. Indeed, with the high unemployment rates that most Western European nations have been experiencing in the 1990s, it would be difficult to say that their respective labour markets are sustaining any efficiency gains from immigration. A realistic appraisal would indicate that precisely the opposite is occurring.

Likewise, the extensive current usage of foreign contract workers in the Near East and in Libya as a means of acquiring needed workers on an extended basis has been rejected by the past experiences of the United States and by Western Europe (Bohning, 1984, Chapters 5 and 6). As there is little prospect that such non-immigrant workers will ever be allowed to become permanent residents of these countries, it can be anticipated that illegal immigration will mount and, over time, there will be tendencies towards political instability in these nations as the economic and social distances between the 'ins' and the 'outs' widens within their populations.

Equity

One of the more significant social trends in the economic development of the advanced industrial nations in the 20th century has been the incorporation of equity concerns into the formulation and evaluation of public policy initiatives. 'Who benefits' and 'who loses' as a consequence of governmental interventions into domestic labour markets are questions that are crucial to any overall assessment of the merits of a particular undertaking.

Equity issues involve not only how immigration policy affects the short-term state of affairs but how does it fit into longer-term efforts by the present generation to correct inequities caused by the actions of past generations. Too much of contemporary economic analysis (i.e., the neoclassical paradigm) is ahistorical in its quest to interpret and to quantify labour market happenings. But once equity considerations are raised, the rationale for policy actions shifts to including the relevant societal circumstances that exist at a specific time.

As previously noted, the traditional use of immigration by most nations has been as a means to supply unskilled labour either as permanent settlers or as temporary workers. The oil-exporting nations, as do some of the rapidly developing nations of Asia, still pursue this course. Since the revival of immigration by the United States, Canada and Australia in the post-1960s era and the termination of temporary worker programmes in Western Europe in the mid-1970s, however, the explicit use of immigration to recruit unskilled workers by these nations has virtually ceased. The employment-based portions of their immigration systems tend to be restricted to admitting only more highly educated and skilled workers. But when allowances are made for the other aspects of their admission systems (family reunification and refugee provisions) as well as the toleration of the mass abuse of these systems by illegal immigration, the picture quickly changes. The preponderance of the entrants resemble, in terms of their human capital characteristics, the traditional immigration pattern: unskilled and poorly educated persons, who often do not speak the native language.

Thus, the equity dimension of contemporary immigration policy focuses on the segment of the labour force that is most impacted by the overall flow of immigrants: the low-skilled segment of the native-born labour force who disproportionately hold or seek jobs in the secondary labour market. It is they who carry most of the accommodation burden. Many of these persons are women, youth and minorities for whom other public policy measures – especially in the United States – ostensibly manifest a concern. The impact of immigration on the well-being of these groups, however, seldom enters the realm of debate over the effects of immigration policy.

In the United States real family incomes have been falling steadily since 1973 and they have fallen the most for low-income families (Peterson, 1991). Real wages have also been declining over this same time span and they have declined the most for low-skilled workers (Bound and Johnson, 1992). National unemployment rates have remained high (when compared to previous periods of prosperity – in the low 6 per cent range in 1994). Sectorial unemployment rates in central cities and in the six states (California, New York, Texas, Florida, Illinois and New Jersey) most heavily impacted by immigration regularly exceed the national rate. Unemployment rates are the highest for those with the lowest levels of educational attainment (the usual proxy used to measure skill). Thus, there is no indication of the existence of any general shortage of labour and absolutely no shortage of unskilled labour in particular that would warrant the level and type of immigration that the United States is sustaining.

Historically, the group in the United States most adversely affected by large-scale immigration has been the black population. Given the legacy of slavery and of *de jure* segregation, the economic welfare of black Americans virtually defines the notion of equity when assessing the efficacy of any public policy initiative. Yet, somehow, immigration policy has been allowed to escape the imperative to meet this crucial test.

The black population was positioned to have been incorporated into the economic mainstream of the United States after being freed from slavery in 1865. The US economy was just entering its industrialization phase in which a vast number and array of new industries and occupations were created. Most of these jobs in manufacturing, construction, mining and transportation were of an unskilled nature. The blacks were unskilled and they were already in the United States (albeit mostly in the South). The most influential spokesman for black America at the time was the noted educator, Booker T. Washington. In his famous Atlanta Exposition speech of 1895, he pleaded with the white industrialists of the nation to draw on the abundantly available native-born black population to fill these nation-building jobs in order to 'make the interests of both races one' (Washington, 1965, p. 147). He warned in a Cassandra-like fashion that the failure to do so would cause the future black population of the nation to become 'a veritable body of death, stagnating, depressing, retarding every effort to advance the body politic' (Washington, 1965, p. 148). His words were not heeded. Waves of immigrants from Eastern and Southern Europe were sought and they poured into the urban labour markets of the North and the West. It was not until this immigration ended in 1914 that the black population could finally begin to migrate out of the South. Every decade since, there was a positive net migration of blacks out of the South – that is until the 1980s. As indicated earlier, the decade of the 1980s saw immigration soar to its highest level in the nation's history and it also witnessed a negative net migration of blacks out of the South for the first time in the 20th century. Reflecting on the historical pattern, Raymond Frost has written that 'there is a competitive relationship between immigration and black migration out of the South .... When the rate of immigration declines, black migration to the North and West increases; when the rate of immigration increases, black migration declines' (Frost, 1991, p. 64 and *New York Times*, 1991, p. A–7). In the present context, blacks are once more losing in the competition for jobs in the urban North and West.

The revival of mass immigration to the United States has had completely unexpected consequences on the development of the Civil Rights Movement in the United States. Beginning in earnest in the South in the late 1950s, the Movement reached its zenith with the passage of historic legislation in 1964 (regarding public accommodation and employment), in 1965 (regarding voting rights), and in 1968 (regarding fair housing). Although the legislation embraced the need to protect other groups as well, the impetus for these laws was directed towards the treatment of black Americans. But what is often overlooked in reviewing the evolution of the Civil Rights movement is that the pathbreaking laws of the 1960s were enacted at a time when immigration levels were at historic lows and entry was sharply limited. With regard to the employment implications of the civil rights laws of the 1960s, the assumption was that they would reduce future discriminatory practices and that they would also be accompanied by other human resource development policies designed to redress the past denial of opportunities for victim groups to be prepared to qualify for jobs. In the short run, this is, in fact, what occurred. Simultaneous legislation was adopted pertaining to education, training, health, housing, community development and poverty prevention. With unemployment declining in the mid-1960s, it was assumed that the newly protected groups – blacks in particular – would soon become qualified to fill the available jobs that a tightening labour market was providing (unemployment rates in the mid-1960s were in the 3 per cent range).

There was no recognition at the time that the parallel reforms in the nation's immigration system that were manifested by the Immigration Act of 1965 were in any way linked to the happenings in the civil rights arena. For as the floor manager of the legislation, Senator Edward M. Kennedy, stated during the final floor debate, 'this bill is not concerned with increasing immigration to this country, nor will it lower any of the high standards we apply in selection of immigrants' (US Congress, 1965, pp. 24, 225). Neither of his assertions proved valid. As indicated earlier, this legislation (and other expansive measures that followed) led to the largest increase in immigration in US history and it is still going on. Moreover, most of the new immigrants have been unskilled, poorly educated, non-English-speaking persons. In the process, policies designed to bring black America into the nation's economic mainstream were undermined. The new immigrants poured into many of the same urban centres where the black population was already concentrated. They became an alternative source of labour – just as immigrants at the turn of the Century had been earlier. In the process, their presence has greatly lessened the need to address the economic plight of black Americans. It has also greatly increased the competition for jobs (especially in the secondary labour market) and for the scarce education and training funds available to overcome the chronic human capital deficiencies of the needy people of all races concentrated in these urban centers.

Since the return of mass immigration, there are clear signs that the economic status of black Americans has deteriorated. Black unemployment rates have risen since the 1960s and are consistently twice the white rates. The black male labour force participation rate has fallen relative to white males. In 1993, the white male participation rate exceeded the black male rate by 7.5 percentage points (76.1 per cent to 68.6 per cent). The wide gap exists for every age sub-grouping. Indicative of the significance of this decline in black male participation is the fact that the absolute number of black women in the labour force in the 1990s exceeds that of black men. Blacks are the only racial group in the US labour force where this phenomenon occurs and the difference is projected by the US Department of Labor to worsen throughout the 1990s.

Aside from the rural South, the nation's black population is disproportionately concentrated in the central cities of 12 major cities outside the South, as well as in the central cities of the South. Jobs in these urban locations are frequently scarce. Moreover, black male workers have been disproportionately displaced by the decline in manufacturing industries and production-related occupations that has occurred since the 1960s because they were disproportionately employed in these sectors (Kletzer, 1991; and Briggs, 1992, Chapter 8). In urban centres, therefore, unskilled immigrants and unskilled blacks have had to compete for the shrinking number of unskilled jobs that remain.

As to the link between immigration and the economic well-being of blacks, it should be noted that 24 per cent of the foreign-born population of the nation in 1990 lived in only seven cities. These cities and the percentage of their respective populations who are foreign born in 1990 are as follows: New York (28 per cent); Los Angeles (38 per cent); Chicago (17 per cent); Houston (18 per cent); San Francisco (34 per cent); San Diego (21 per cent); and Miami (60 per cent). With the exception of San Diego, each of these cities also have substantial black populations.

Competition from immigrants is not the only factor to explain the high black unemployment rate and the low black male labour force participation rate but it must be included within any such list of negative influences. The adverse impact has been highlighted by studies of the 1992 urban riots in Los Angeles, California – the worst race riots the country has ever sustained (Miles, 1992; Reinhold, 1991, p. A–20; Royce, 1991, p. A–1; and Reinhold, 1992, p. E–1). Specific case-studies are rare but one in southern California clearly documented the situation whereby black janitorial workers, who had successfully built a strong union in the 1970s that provided high wages and good working conditions, were almost totally displaced by Hispanic immigrants in the 1980s who were willing to work as non-union employees for far lower pay and with few benefits (Mines and Avina, 1992).

Studies of the New York City labour market, which has the highest absolute number of foreign-born persons of any city in the nation, have found that immigrant workers are clustered into only a few industries. Almost half (47 per cent) of all post-965 immigrants were employed in only 13 industries – out of over 200 for which Census data are collected (Bogen, 1987, p. 84; and Bouvier and Briggs, 1988, Chapter 8). These industries, however, accounted for an incredible 35 per cent of all employed persons in the city. The preponderance of the post-1965 foreign-born-workers were concentrated in generally low-paying industries such as apparel manufacturing, hospitals, eating and drinking establishments, private household work, hotels and nursing facilities.

There is also evidence that some immigrants, who themselves become employers and who have opened their own businesses in urban cities, actively discriminate against native-born workers – especially blacks – in their hiring practices. In her study of immigrants in New York City, Elizabeth Bogen candidly described the phenomenon: 'there are tens of thousands of jobs in New York City for which the native born are not candidates' (Bogen, 1987, p. 91). The reasons she cites are that 'ethnic hiring networks and the proliferation of immigrant-owned small businesses in the city have cut off open-market competition for jobs' and that the blatant 'discrimination against native workers is a matter for future monitoring'. (Bogen, 1987, p. 81). Even research in those rural labour markets where immigrant workers have become a significant factor (e.g., in the agriculture industry of the Southwest) has revealed the widespread use of ethnic networking which dominates the hiring process (Mines and Martin, 1984). The negative effect of immigrant-hiring networks on the employment of native-born workers in these rural areas is the same in its consequences as it is in urban labour markets. The concept of networking is highly praised by many scholars who study the current immigrant experience (Portes and Rumbaut, 1990). But what is overlooked is that these hiring practices – the use of national origin as a factor to favor or to deny employment opportunities – are specifically banned by the Civil Rights Act of 1964. What was legally permissible at the beginning of the 20th century is illegal at its end. So far, however, no government agency has been willing to pursue the issue of discrimination by immigrants against native-born Americans – especially if they are black citizens.

Immigration is also having another more subtle effect on equity issues in the United States. Namely, due to its scale and composition, immigration is rapidly changing the balance of political power in those cities and states that have been receiving most of the post-1965 immigrants. No racial group since the United States achieved its independence has received fewer new members as immigrants than has the black population. When the 19th century began, blacks constituted about 20 per cent of the US population. By the end of the 19th century, the mass immigration of Europeans and Asians had led to the reduction in the proportion of the black population to about 10 per cent. Throughout the 20th Century, there has been little increase in the black population as the result of immigration (Passel and Edmonston, 1992). As noted earlier, the preponderance of the post-1965 immigration to the United States has been of people who presently constitute other minority groups – Hispanics and Asians. There have been relatively few blacks among their numbers. Thus, one of the most dramatic effects of post-1965 immigration has been to create a significant shift in the make-up of the nation's minority population. The 1990 Census revealed that, for the first time in US history, the black population accounts for less than half of the nation's minority population (Passel and Edmonston, 1992, p. 6). Looking ahead to the 21st century, it can be anticipated that this shift will 'have profound implications for political and social relations among race/ethnic groups in the United States' (Passel and Edmonston, 1992, p. 6).

Under most circumstances, the fact that the racial and ethnic composition of the United States is changing would not warrant concern for policy changes to avoid such an outcome. But the economic welfare and the social status of blacks in the United States is a special case. The historical treatment of blacks has placed special obligations on succeeding generations of Americans to try to right the wrongs of the past. There may be legitimate disagreements among Americans over the extent to which such a correction can be achieved by public policy interventions into labour markets; but certainly no discretionary element of public policy should be allowed to inflict harm upon black Americans in their quest for equality of opportunity. Unfortunately, post-1965 immigration policy cannot pass that test. Indeed, it has been inimical to the achievement of that goal. To be sure, this was not the intention of immigration reformers in the 1960s or of pro-immigration supporters over the subsequent years. But to allow the prevailing immigration system to continue to function without regard for its adverse effects on blacks can only lead to one conclusion: immigration policy has once more become a form of institutional racism. It has provided a way to avoid addressing the dire economic plight of black Americans.

To date, equity considerations have been ignored in the design and the assessment of the nation's post-1965 revival of mass immigration. The adverse consequences of this omission have fallen most severely on unskilled workers in general but on black workers in particular because they are, unfortunately, concentrated in the unskilled labour market and often in the same geographic labour markets most highly impacted by immigration.

In the case of Canada, equity is an issue but far less so than in the United States. In the past, the use of the point system and the flexibility in the annual immigration ceiling has made its system more accountable for its economic consequences than in the United States. Nonetheless, as the number of immigrants admitted on the basis of family ties and as refugees has increased and with immigration levels in the 1990s reaching unprecedented levels despite rising unemployment, equity concerns about the impact on unskilled workers bear careful monitoring in the coming years (Reimers and Troper, 1992, pp. 19–25 and 32–8). It is a latent issue.

Immigration has, at times, become ensnared in Canada's timeless dispute between its charter ethnic groups, the British and the French. But once Canada decided to adopt an active policy of recruitment of immigrants in the post-World War II era, it was not long before Canada followed the lead of the United States by enacting legislation in 1967 that removed discriminatory barriers from its entry system. In the succeeding years, the number of immigrants who are neither of British nor French heritage has risen dramatically – especially with immigrants from Asia, Africa and Latin America (Sullivan, 1992, p. 162). But without the legacy of slavery and *de jure* segregation, Canada's immigration system has not been as plagued by the equity concerns about differential impacts on native born racial groups as has the United States.

As for the receiving countries in Western Europe, the major equity issues are far less obvious since the era of reliance on guestworkers ended in 1973. Those programmes have been soundly criticized on equity grounds by W.R. Bohning who described their demise as being due to the fact that they were 'not only morally offensive but politically less and less tenable' for Western European democracies (Bohning, 1984, p. 162). Ray Rist, for instance, contended that the guestworker programmes created a marginal segment of the labour force in the receiving countries of workers who were only useful as long as there was no attempt to improve their working and living conditions or to incorporate them into the economic mainstream of the respective host countries (Rist, 1979).

Since 1973, as discussed earlier, the member nations of the

European Union have sought to reduce immigration from non-member nations while increasing labour mobility between EU members. The adoption of the Single European Act in December 1985 (which became effective in 1993) sought to codify this position. Given the high unemployment that continues to characterize most EU nations and the spread of long-term unemployment among its member work forces, this course of action is logical (Bean, 1994). The EU countries no longer need an infusion of unskilled workers. Hence, when faced with a choice of 'a very restrictive immigration policy or ... a more liberal one which is racist' (i.e., an employment-based policy that favours only immigrants who speak the native language of the receiving country and who already have needed skills, talents and education), they have chosen the former (Whitney, 1991, p. A-8). The EU nations will, however, still be confronted with the legacy issues that are the residual effects of their guestworker programmes – family reunification and illegal immigration. The associated equity issues, therefore, will centre on equal access to jobs and job preparation for their foreign-born populations as well as with citizenship rights and cultural assimilation issues. The entry question, it seems, has been decided: Western Europe no longer desires to be a receiving region. The dilemma of how Europe will handle continuing illegal immigration and the ongoing surge of economic refugees masquerading as political asylum applicants, it seems, will determine the fate of access and treatment of future immigrants.

Effects on Social Policy

Western Europe has led the world in the development of social policies that are designed to smooth over the hard edges of free market economies for workers and their families. Competitive economic systems breed winners and losers, by definition. The maintenance of full employment for prolonged periods has proved to be difficult. Under these circumstances, most Western European countries have concluded that income guarantees for families with children, health care, school-to-work transition programmes, support for unions, and liberal unemployment compensation programmes are obligations that require societal responses. Canada has tended to resemble Europe in its adherence to these beliefs and the establishment of similar protective programmes. As for the United States, it has been less willing to acknowledge the fact that free markets have problems that dictate social solutions. But, in fact, it has tended to follow Western European leadership in most vital areas of social policy but, usually, with great reluctance and considerable time lapses. Some social policies – such as the provision of universal health care and child allowances – are still resisted.

These social policies, however, are expensive. Their continuation and adequacy depends on the ability to keep their costs from becoming prohibitive. As long as immigration levels were low, the benefits of the welfare state were not threatened and the immigrants were usually included with a minimum of opposition. But as suggested by Becker, these social programmes can serve as a human magnet to poor people in less developed countries to emigrate from their homelands. Indeed, they may be as powerful in their attraction powers as are the opportunities for possible employment that emanate from the job market of the receiving nations. When immigration is perceived to be 'out of control' (as a presidential commission in the United States has found it to be), the cost of providing human services to immigrants and refugees can undermine the tenuous support and possibly even the continuation of the social policies of these receiving nations. They can also hinder efforts to enhance these programmes by providing higher benefits and wider coverage in response to worsening domestic economic conditions (in Western Europe and in Canada) and fiscal stress (in the United States) in the 1990s.

In the United States, support by special interest groups for higher levels of immigration and for weak deterrence measures against illegal immigration has been based on alleged benefits that accrue by these developments. They have conscientiously eschewed discussions of the associated costs. Immigration advocates had their way in the 1980s. But, given the anomaly of the immigration policy process in the United States (whereby immigration policy is the exclusive prerogative of the federal government but most of the actual adjustment costs fall on local and state governments), the issue of costs had to be faced eventually. The local and state governments where immigrants have congregated have manifested a groundswell of protest as they have struggled to pay the mounting financial obligations of immigration. In 1994, for example, the Governor of California charged that immigration was costing his state $3 billion annually and he filed a suit against the federal government for partial compensation of the cost of incarceration of criminal aliens ($1.6 billion) and for providing health costs to illegal aliens ($369 million); San Diego County, California, filed a suit for an additional $59 million to cover the costs of criminal incarceration; the Governor of Florida released a report claiming that illegal immigration was costing his state $884 million for the provision of education, health and incarceration; the New York State Senate released a report claiming that immigration was annually costing the state $5.6 billion for social services, incarceration and education, and announced it would begin negotiations with the federal government for reimbursement of these expenses; a study in Texas placed the annual costs of legal and illegal immigrants at $4.6 billion for its governmental services; and the Attorney General of Arizona filed a federal suit for $121 million for reimbursement for the cost of criminal incarcerations (*San Jose Mercury News*, 1994, p. 1; Office of the Governor of Florida, 1994; New York State Senate, 1994; Beachy, 1994, p. A-1; and *Washington Times*, 1994, p. 1). Other states are considering similar actions. These suits are only the tip of the iceberg. The actual costs of mass immigrant accommodation have yet to be fully exposed. For example, it is estimated that two million immigrant children enrolled in US public schools in the 1980s. Studies of these immigrant children indicate that they are 'twice as likely to be poor as compared to all students, thereby straining local school resources' and that 'many immigrants, including those of high school age, have had little or no schooling and are illiterate even in their native languages' (US General Accounting Office, 1994, p. 2). New demands for the creation of bilingual programmes and special education classes have added to the costs of education and have frequently led to the diversion of funds from other important programmes for other needy children. Overcrowding of urban schools, already confronting enormous educational burdens, has frequently occurred with devastating impacts on the educational process (Firestone, 1994, p. A-1). Other educational costs to social policy are more subtle but equally significant as financial concerns. Namely, the societal goal of desegregated urban schools has been greatly retarded by the arrival of immigrant children because it has increased the racial isolation of inner-city black children (Fiske, 1988, p. A-16).

Even the federal government itself has entered the fray over costs by reporting that elderly legal immigrants, who entered under family reunification provisions and who did not work in the United States so they do not qualify for Social Security benefits, are annually costing the federal government $1.2 billion in food stamps and Supplemental Security Income benefits (*Migration News*, 1994, p. 2). Research has also disclosed that immigrants in the 1980s made greater use of the federal-state welfare programme for dependent children than did native born citizens (Borjas and Trejo, 1991). In addition, the issue of coverage for illegal immigrants under the national health-care programme proposed by the Clinton Administration in 1994 became a major point of contention to an already controversial proposal, as did the issue of the eligibility of children of illegal immigrants under the Administration's proposed welfare reforms (Anderson, 1994; and Verhovek, 1994, p. A-1).

Thus, there is a quandary developing in each of the receiving nations. As the number of immigrants – a disproportionate number of whom are poor – enter these countries, the costs of accommodating them in the social programmes of these nations are disproportionately increased. In the wake of rising costs, there is pressure to exclude needy immigrants. But such actions would create an untenable two-tiered society that is likely to have significant intergenerational effects. Another alternative is to retain the existing programmes but reduce benefit levels and restrict coverage for everyone, but this too is arbitrary and cruel. It, too, would widen the income gap between 'haves' and 'have nots' and be socially divisive. This leaves only one remaining option: reform immigration policies by making them accountable for their economic and social consequences. Western Europe has chosen this last option. In the United States and Canada, the choice remains to be made but the day of reckoning does not seem far away.

CONCLUDING OBSERVATIONS

From the vantage point of the receiving countries, the planned immigration component of international labour migration is limited and situation-specific. Few countries currently are willing to admit immigrants. Those that do, have been willing to do so under proscribed terms and with set limits. The admissions are based largely on non-economic, political considerations. But, as the economic consequences of these political policies have begun to surface and to

be recognized as being significant in scale, support for immigration
for permanent settlement has waned. Contraction has already begun
in Western Europe. In Canada and the United States, planned
immigration remains high, but it has become a subject of contentious
debate with the future outcome uncertain. In Australia, levels of
immigration have been reduced while arguments over the proper
admission criteria continue.

Faced with 'stress' in their domestic economies, which is
symbolized by high unemployment and caused by the introduction of
new labour-displacing technologies and the reduction of international
trade barriers, employers are rapidly readjusting their production
systems. The employment responses to these changes have revealed
significant labour market mismatches between the types of skilled and
educated workers that are needed and the supply of unskilled workers
that are not (Friedman, 1994, p. D-1). Structural unemployment of
this nature is not amenable to conventional fiscal and monetary
remedies. In this economic environment, labour market policies come
to the forefront. Immigration, which is a discretionary element of each
nation's labour policies, has come under particular scrutiny. None of
the receiving nations need more unskilled workers. But, given the
political nature of their existing immigration policies (i.e., the
admission of family reunification immigrants, diversity immigrants
and refugees), it is unskilled workers that dominate the overall inflow
into their respective labour forces.

All of the countries that are receiving immigrants for permanent
settlement have liberal welfare systems in place. Confronted with the
imperative to create jobs for their unemployed while striving to protect
the integrity of their social welfare policies, it is not surprising that
there would be resistance to immigration policies that add to the
eligibility pools, necessitate increased social expenditures, and add to
the ranks of the unemployed (Ireland, 1994; and Verhovek, 1994, p.
A-1).

But, aside from the direct cost issues, there is also the fact that the
job competition impact of immigration is grossly uneven. It is not the
better educated and highly skilled segments of the labour force that
bear most of the effects of the competition. Rather, it is the low-
skilled and low-paid workers of each country who bear these burdens.
Disproportionately, these workers tend to be youth, women and
minority group members. The result, therefore, is that immigration

policy in its present form represents a societal imposition of hardship on precisely the segments of the population and labour force that are in the greatest of need of both assistance and protection.

To be sure, many of the immigrants and their families are fleeing circumstances that are often worse than the conditions confronting unskilled citizen workers and their families in the receiving nations. But, adding needy immigrants to the ranks of the needy citizens of these countries raises serious equity concerns. No policy that makes it more difficult to provide adequate job opportunities, health care, education and housing for needy citizens can possibly be in the national interest of any nation – even if the immigrants themselves are better off in these countries than if they stayed in their homelands.

As for unplanned (i.e., illegal) immigration, all of these countries that are currently receiving immigrants are experiencing the phenomena – be they unauthorized border crossers, visa 'overstayers', or economic refugees claiming political asylum. The issue of unplanned immigration, however, is not restricted to the few nations who are admitting legal immigrants. It seems to occur on every continent, wherever any one country is better off than are its neighbours. But it is a special problem for the advanced industrial democracies because of the absolute number of people involved and because they attract illegal immigrants from multiple sources, not just neighbouring countries. All of these industrial democracies have taken legislative steps to curtail illegal immigration. But still it continues and, in fact, it increases. David North has succinctly explained why: 'I suggest that democracies do not control international migration well because they are reluctant to devote the needed financial, diplomatic, intellectual, and above all, emotional resources to the issue' (North, 1991, p. 4). Thus, while the industrial democracies do pass laws against illegal immigration, there 'is an articulate and powerful set of interest groups which are not sympathetic to the enforcement of immigration law' (North, 1991, p. 4). Chief among these are certain business groups who hire large numbers of low-skilled workers (e.g., agri-business in the United States). But the coalition also includes influential organizations of ethnic, racial and religious groups who are largely concerned with increasing their numbers rather than the interests of the nation as a whole. They are joined by a growing number of powerful organizations that exist only to serve immigrants and refugees and whose institutional existence depends entirely on a continuation of immigrant flows. The collective influence of these entities keeps immigration enforcement a low priority issue. To be effective, as North indicates, far more funds are needed to make the existing laws work than the governments of the receiving nations are presently willing to appropriate; the topic must be given higher diplomatic priority even if the result is an increase in ill-will generated by the governments of the sending countries; more attention needs to be given by immigration scholars to nitty-gritty issues pertaining to the actual means of law enforcement; and the receiving nations must overcome the feeling of emotional guilt about sending violators back to their homelands in order to discourage even a greater number from coming in the future. Although North is pessimistic about the prospects of the industrial democracies taking these steps, he clearly articulates the imperative for doing so:

> The big losers are the disadvantaged legal workers, often of minority origin, who either lose their jobs to newcomers, or, more often, find their wages and working conditions depressed because of the presence of newcomers in a specific segment of the labour market .... If the State provides welfare benefits to the displaced domestic workers, then taxpayers are lesser losers as well. (North, 1991, p. 5)

Thus, there is an anomaly in any effort to appraise the international labour mobility aspects of global immigration on receiving nations. On the one hand, the planned immigration component of such movements is limited to access to only a handful of countries whose numbers are diminishing; on the other hand, unplanned immigration – in all of its forms – shows every sign of expansion. Consequently, the net effect is likely to be that international migration will increase in the future despite formal efforts to reduce it.

The scale of international labour migration, therefore, will more likely be determined by what is happening in the sending countries than in the receiving nations. The economic problems confronting the sending countries, which cause so many of their people to leave, are immense and the prospect is that they will worsen. But, to the degree that humane solutions for their plight do exist, out-migration cannot be one of them. For aside from the adverse effects on the receiving countries, out-migration alone does nothing to resolve the fundamental causes of the problems in their homelands. Until they are addressed directly, the 'push' factors in the sending countries will simply go on indefinitely. If the 'have' countries of the world want to help, they must address the systemic causes of distress in those countries whose leaders themselves want to change these conditions. Fundamental to the success of any such effort is the acceptance of the need for population planning and control measures. The 'have' nations could provide the information and the contraceptive means to limit family size and to reduce population growth. They can also provide the technical and the economic assistance needed to develop the education and training of their work forces as well as the production expertise needed to diversify their existing industrial bases so as to introduce new industries and to expand domestic job opportunities. They can also adopt trade policies that provide access to the sending nations to export to their countries. The advanced industrial countries should link the provision of economic assistance and trade concessions to assurances by the governments of these countries that they will strictly adhere to international human rights and human liberty standards. And, lastly, the receiving countries should resist the temptation to 'brain drain' the sending countries of the talent they need to develop their economies. Pursuit of these international policies is far more preferable, in terms of desirable outcomes, than is the option of expanding international labour migration itself or the option of doing nothing.

REFERENCES

Anderson, Annelise (1994), 'What Should Our Immigration Policy Be?', *Modern Thought*, p. 364-9.

Asch, Beth J. (1994), *Emigration and Its Effects on the Sending Countries*, Santa Monica, CA: Rand Corporation.

Beachy, Debra (1994), 'Study Estimates Immigrants Cost Texas $4.68 Billion in 1992', *The Houston Chronicle*, 3 March.

Bean, Charles R. (1994), 'European Unemployment: A Survey', *Journal of Economic Literature*, 32 (2), pp. 573-619.

Becker, Gary S. (1992), 'An Open Door for Immigrants – the Auction', *Wall Street Journal*, 14 October.

Birrell, R. (1984), 'A New Era in Australian Migration Policy',

International Migration Review, 18 (1), pp. 65–84.

Bogen, Elizabeth (1987), *Immigration in New York*, New York: Praeger.

Bohning, W.R. (1984), *Studies in International Labor Migration*, London: The Macmillan Press.

Borjas, George (1990), *Friends or Strangers: The Impact of Immigration on the U.S. Economy*, New York: eg. Basic Books, Inc.

Borjas, George, Richard Freeman and Lawrence Katz (1992), 'On the Labor Market Effects of Immigration and Trade', in George Borjas and Richard Freeman (eds), *Immigration and the Work Force*, Chicago: University of Chicago Press, pp. 213–44.

Borjas, George and Stephen J. Trejo (1991), 'Immigrant Participation in the Welfare System', *Industrial and Labor Relations Review*, 44 (2), pp. 195–211.

Bound, John and George Johnson (1992), 'Changes in the Structure of Wages in the 1980s: An Evaluation of Alternative Explanations', *American Economic Review*, 82 (3), pp. 371–92.

Bouvier, Leon and Vernon M. Briggs, Jr. (1988), *The Population and Labor Force of New York: 1990 to 2050*, Washington, DC: The Population Reference Bureau.

Briggs, Vernon M., Jr. (1984), *Immigration Policy and the American Labor Force*, Baltimore: The Johns Hopkins University Press.

Briggs, Vernon M., Jr. (1992), *Mass Immigration and the National Interest*, Armonk, NY: M.E. Sharpe, Inc.

Briggs, Vernon M., Jr. (1993), 'Immigrant Labor and The Issue of "Dirty Work" in Advanced Industrial Societies', *Population and Environment*, 14 (6), pp. 503–14.

Briggs, Vernon M., Jr. (1995), 'Mass Immigration, Free Trade, and the Forgotten American Worker', in Lydio Tomasi (ed.), *In Defense of the Alien*, 17, New York, Center for Migration Studies.

Brimelow, Peter (1993), 'The Closed Door', *Social Contract*, 3 (1), pp. 44–5.

Castles, Stephen (1984), *Here for Good: eg. Western Europe's New Ethnic Minorities*, London: Pluto Press.

Castles, Stephen (1989), *Migrant Workers in Western Society*, Ithaca: Cornell University Press.

Center for Immigration Studies (1992), 'Australia' and 'Canada',

Immigration and Nationality Policies of Leading Migration Nations, Washington, DC:. Center for Immigration Studies.

Center for Immigration Studies (undated), 'Israel', Washington, DC (material has not yet been published).

Chiswick, Barry (1986), 'Is the New Immigration Less Skilled Than the Old?', *Journal of Labor Economics*, 4 (2), pp. 192–6.

Clayton, Mark (1994), 'Some Foreigners Need Not Apply Under Canada's Immigration Plan', *The Christian Science Monitor*, 3 November.

Coleman, David A. (1994), 'Ins and Outs of British Migration Policy', *The Social Contract*, 4 (4), pp. 254–60.

Cross, Gary (1983), *Immigrant Workers in Industrial France*, Philadelphia: Temple University Press.

Darnton, John (1993), 'Western Europe is Ending Its Welcome to Immigrants', *New York Times*, 10 August.

Economist, The (1993), 'France: Zero Option', 12 June 12.

Firestone, David (1994), 'Crowded Schools in Queens Find Class Space in Unusual Places', *New York Times*, 8 June.

Fiske, E. (1988), 'Racial Shifts Challenge U.S. Schools', *New York Times*, 23 June.

Friedman, Milton (1962), *Capitalism and Freedom*, Chicago: University of Chicago Press.

Friedman, Milton and Rose Friedman (1990), *Free to Choose: A Personal Statement*, Harcourt, Brace, Janovich.

Friedman, Thomas L. 'Accent on Education as Talks on Jobs End', *New York Times*, 16 March.

Frost, Raymond M. (1991), 'Commentary', *Challenge: The Magazine of Economic Affairs*, November–December.

Ireland, Patrick (1994), *The Challenge of Ethnic Diversity: Immigrant Politics in France and Switzerland*, Cambridg, Mass.: Harvard University Press.

Kinzer, Stephen (1991), 'Germany Agrees on Law to Curb Refugees and Seekers of Asylum', *New York Times*, 8 December.

Kinzer, Stephen (1993), 'Bonn Parliament Votes Sharp Curb on Asylum Seekers', *New York Times*, 27 May.

Kletzer, Lorri G. (1991), 'Job Displacement, 1979–1986: How Blacks Fared Relative to Whites', *Monthly Labor Review*, 114 (7), pp. 17–25.

Lebergott, Stanley (1964), *Manpower in Economic Growth*, New York: McGraw Hill Book Company.

McNeill, William H. (1987), 'Migration in Pre-Modern Times' in William Alonzo (ed.), *Population in an Interacting World*, Cambridge, Mass.: Harvard University Press.

Marcus, Amy D. (1994), 'As the Sick and Aged Head to Israel, Critics Cry "Shut the Door"', *Wall Street Journal*, 31 October.

Martin, Philip L. (1994a), 'Immigration and Integration: Challenges for the 1990s', *Social Contract*, 4 (3), pp. 177-82.

Martin, Philip L. (1994b), 'Comparative Migration Policies', *International Migration Review*, 28 (1), pp. 164-70.

Meisenheimer, J.R. (1992), 'How Do Immigrants Fare in the U.S. Labor Market?', *Monthly Labor Review*, 115 (12), pp. 3-19.

Migration News (1994), 'Eliminating SSI for Immigrants', 1 April.

Miles, Jack (1992), 'Immigration and the New American Dilemma: Black vs. Brown', *The Atlantic*, October, pp. 41-68.

Miller, Mark and Philip Martin (1982), *Administering Foreign Labor Programs*, Lexington, MA: D.C. Heath, Inc.

Mines, Richard and Philip Martin (1984), 'Immigrant Workers and the California Citrus Industry', *Industrial Relations*, 23 (1), pp. 139-49.

Mines, Richard and Jeffrey Avina (1992), 'Immigrants and Labor Standards: The Case of California Janitors', in Jorge A. Bustamante (ed.), *U.S. Mexico Relations: Labor Market Interdependence*, Stanford: Stanford University Press, pp. 429-48.

Morita, Kirro and Saskia Sassen (1994), 'The New Illegal Immigration in Japan, 1980-1992', *International Migration Review*, 28 (1), pp. 153-63.

New York State Senate, Committee on Cities 1994, *Our Teeming Shore: A Legislative Report on The Impact of U.S. Immigration Policy on New York State*, Albany, NY, January.

New York Times, (1991), 'Blacks in Decline in Northern Cities', 6 July.

North, David (1991), 'Why Democratic Governments Cannot Cope With Illegal Immigration', Paper presented at the International Conference on Migration, Rome, Italy, 13-15 March, 1991 sponsored by the Organization for Economic Cooperation and Development.

Office of the Governor of Florida (1994), *The Unfair Burden: Immigration's Impact on Florida*, Tallahasee, Florida, 13 March.

Oxford Analytica (1986), *America in Perspective*, Boston: Houghton-Mifflin.

Passel, Jeffrey and Barry Edmonston (1992), *Immigration and Race in the United States: The 20th and 21st Centuries*, Program for Research on Immigration Policy, PRIP-UI-20, Washington, DC: The Urban Institute.

Peterson, Wallace (1991), 'The Silent Depression', *Challenge: The Magazine of Economic Affairs*, August, pp. 29–34.

Portes, Alejandro and Ruben G. Rumbaut (1990), *Immigrant America*, Berkeley: University of California Press.

Reder, Melvin W. (1963), 'The Economic Consequences of Increased Immigration', *The Review of Economics and Statistics*, 45 (3), pp. 221–30.

Reder, Melvin W. (1982), 'Chicago Economics: Permanence and Change', *Journal of Economic Literature*, 20 (1), pp. 1–38.

Reimers, David M. and Harold Troper (1992), 'Canadian and American Immigration Policy Since 1945', in Barry R. Chiswick (ed.), *Immigration, Language, and Ethnicity: Canada and the United States*, Washington, DC: The American Enterprise Institute, pp. 15–54.

Reinhold, Donald (1991), 'In California, New Talk About a Taboo Subject', *New York Times*, 3 December.

Reinhold, Robert (1992), 'A Terrible Chain of Events Reveals Los Angeles Without Its Makeup', *New York Times*, 3 May, Section 4.

Riding, Alan (1993), 'French Parliament Approves Tighter Immigration Controls', *New York Times*, 14 May.

Rist, Ray (1978), *Guestworkers in Germany: The Prospects for Pluralism*, New York: Praeger Inc.

Rist, Ray (1979),'Migration and Marginality: Guestworkers in Germany and France', *Daedalus*, 108 (2), pp. 95–108.

Royce, Joseph N. (1991), 'Struggle Over Hospital in Los Angeles' Pits Minority Versus Minority', *The Wall Street Journal*, 1 April.

San Jose Mercury News (1994), 'Wilson Sues U.S. to Recoup Immigrants Health Costs', 31 May.

Schumpeter, Joseph A. (1954), *History of Economic Analysis*, New York: Oxford University Press.

Simon, Julian L. (1991), 'The Case for Greatly Increased Immigration', *The Public Interest*, 102, pp. 89–103.

Simons, Henry C. (1948), *Economic Policy for a Free Society*, Chicago: University of Chicago Press.

Sterngold, James (1989), 'Japan Curbing Foreign Workers', *New York Times*, 12 December.

Sullivan, Teresa A. (1992), 'The Changing Demographic Characteristics and Impact of Immigrants in Canada', in Barry Chiswick (ed.), *Immigrants, Language, and Ethnicity: Canada and the United States*, Washington, DC: The American Enterprise Institute, pp. 119–44.

United Nations Population Fund (1993), *The State of World Population: 193*, New York: eg. United Nations Population Fund.

US Codes, 'Immigration and Nationality Act' (with Amendments), 8 (212).

US Congress, Senate (1965), *Congressional Record*.

US General Accounting Office (1994), *Immigrant Education*, Statement of Linda Morra, Director of Education and Employment Issues, Health Education and Human Services Division to US Senate Committee on Labor and Human Resources, 14 April, 1994, GAO/T-HEHS-94-1946.

van de Kaa, Dirk, J. (1993), 'European Migration at the End of History', *European Review*, 1 (1), pp. 87–108.

Verhovek, Sam H. (1994), 'Stop Benefits for Aliens? It Wouldn't Be That Easy', *New York Times*, 8 June.

Waldman, Peter (1993), 'Algerians See France as a Betrayer, Closing Immigration Door on Old Colony', *Wall Street Journal*, 11 June.

Wall Street Journal, The (1989), 'The Re-Kindled Flame', 3 July.

Washington, Booker T. (1965), 'The Atlanta Exposition Address', *Up from Slavery* as reprinted in *Three Negro Classics*, New York: Avon Books, 1965.

Washington Times, (1994), 'Arizona Sues for Costs of Aliens', 3 May.

Whitney, Craig R. (1991), 'Europeans Look for Ways to Bar Door to Immigrants', *New York Times*, 29 December.

4 Economic Integration and Migration: The European Case

Heinz Werner

BACKGROUND

The following chapter describes how European economic integration has developed since the foundation of the European Economic Community (EEC) in 1957 – later renamed the European Community (EC) – and what consequences this has had for the migration of labour between the Member States. How did the advancement of economic and regional integration in Western Europe affect the migration of labour between the Member States? What lessons does the EC experience teach about the effect of regional integration upon intra-EC migration? Would any further expansion of the European Union towards the North and the East yield analogous results? We can start to shed some light on these questions by outlining the development of the European Community (EC), which has now evolved into the European Union (EU). This is followed by a description of migration movements since the introduction of the free movement of labour and finally by an overview of the determinants of the migration of labour. The parallel economic European integration over this time period is analysed against the backdrop of this migration. The comparison of the migration flows with the development of European integration could then be used to explain the flows as well as the future expected migration of labour in Europe. The final chapter shows the contours of a European immigration policy.

The EEC was founded in 1957 upon the signing of the Treaty of Rome. Signatory states were France, the Federal Republic of Germany, Italy, Belgium, the Netherlands and Luxembourg. In 1973 the United Kingdom, Ireland and Denmark joined, followed by Greece in 1981 and Spain and Portugal in 1986. From the outset, the agenda of the EC included the idea of fostering the political community through socio-economic integration. While Europeans differ on the ultimate and preferable nature of the European Union, this avowed goal clearly sets the EC off against free trade areas like the recently established North American Free Trade Agreement (NAFTA).

In 1968 the customs union was completed. Customs duties and quantitative trade restrictions – such as quotas – were abolished between the Member States and a common external tariff was introduced. Even in the absence of customs duties and quotas many obstacles still impede the inter-state exchange of goods or capital. These obstacles consist, for example, of technical standards for goods varying from country to country or of different currency regulations for the movement of capital. A truly European common market requires the realization of the four 'basic freedoms': the unimpeded cross-border movement of goods, services, capital and labour. Hence the EC Commission strove to reduce such impediments which hamper transactions and distort competition. It called for harmonized and Community-wide policies, for example uniform trade and competition policies. Distortions of competition resulting from national non-tariff obstacles such as technical standards or national subsidies, which have not been coordinated throughout the Community, are inadmissible.

The Single European Act of 1986 laid the foundation for the creation of the Single European Market by 1993. The following measures were envisaged:

- abolition of border controls for persons and goods;
- harmonization of standards and technical regulations;
- allowing services to be offered everywhere in the Community on the same terms – including the services of banks, insurances;
- harmonization of consumer taxes, particularly of value added tax;
- Europe-wide invitations to tender for public orders above a certain financial level;
- extension of the freedom of movement ruling to persons not in gainful employment and facilitation of intra-Community mobility, e.g. by mutual recognition of qualifications;

This ambitious programme has largely been realized.

Meanwhile all EC countries ratified the Maastricht Treaty for the creation of a European Union. From an economic point of view, the very heart of this treaty are the provisions for a European economic and monetary union. It is envisaged that – at the latest by 1999 – the transition to a uniform currency and to an independent European central bank committed to the aim of price stability will have taken place. At the moment it seems doubtful whether this time schedule can be kept, due to the uncertainties in the monetary system and the still disparate financial and economic policies of the Member States.

MIGRATION OF LABOUR IN THE EUROPEAN COMMUNITY

The Effect of Free Movement of Labour in Practice

Free movement of labour, i.e. the opportunity to look for employment in another EC country and to hold it just as any national of that country, has been a reality for the six founding members – France, Italy, the Federal Republic of Germany, Belgium, the Netherlands and Luxembourg – since 1968.[1] It now applies to all of the 12 member countries. Thus it is one of the major achievements of European integration.

When free movement of labour was under discussion in the 1960s, there were fears that Italian workers would flood the labour market.[2] At that time, Italy was the major European emigration country. But the tide of Italian workers never came. The employment of Italian workers in the EC did, in fact, increase, but Italian migration grew less than the average for EC members as a whole between 1962 and 1972.

Nor did the accession of the United Kingdom, Ireland and Denmark in 1973 prompt a wave of migration and the same applied to full free movement of labour for Greek workers in 1987. There is no reason to expect developments with Spain and Portugal to be any different. The transition period to full free movement of labour for these states expired on 1 January 1993.

Table 4.1 shows the development of the foreign population and foreign work force in the EC Member States.

Table 4.1: **Foreign population and foreign employees in EC countries in thousands**

Foreign population/ foreign employees		Belgium	Denmark	Germany	Greece	Spain
Foreign population total	1975	–	94	4.090	–	165
	1980	879(a)	100	4.453	70	183
	1985	898	108	4.379	98	242
	1986	–	117	4.513	106	293
	1987	–	–	4.241	121	335
	1988	859	136	4.489	155	–
	1989	869	142	4.846	173	398
	1990	881	151	5.242(c)	172	408
	1991	905	161	5.343	184	408
of which: EC countries	1975	–	–	1.616	–	93
	1980	598(a)	25	1.503	19	108
	1985	584	26	1.357	30	142
	1986	–	27	1.365	34	170
	1987	–	–	1.240	38	193
	1988	537	27	1.276	46	–
	1989	537	27	1.325	50	231
	1990	541	27	1.422(c)	50	241
	1991	552	28	1.439	54	241
of which: non-EC countries	1975	–	–	2.474	–	72
	1980	281(a)	75	2.950	52	75
	1985	314	82	3.022	68	98
	1986	–	91	3.148	74	122
	1987	–	–	3.000	83	140
	1988	322	109	3.213	109	–
	1989	322	115	3.250	123	166
	1990	340	124	3.819(c)	122	167
	1991	353	133	3.904	130	167
Foreign employees total	1975	230	41	2.091	-	–
	1980	213	39(a)	2.041	25	59
	1985	187	39	1.555	24	–
	1986	–	43	1.547	24	-
	1987	177	46	1.557	25	-
	1988	179	47	1.577	24	–
	1989	196	47	1.646	22	50
	1990	–	47	1.740	23	63
	1991	–	47	1.842	30	76
	1992	–	45	1.967	-	168
of which: EC countries	1975	174	14	849	–	-
	1980	159	11(a)	732	5	31
	1985	141	12	520	6	28(b)
	1986	–	12	498	7	-
	1987	130	13	484	7	-
	1988	131	13	473	6	-
	1989	141	13	483	7	24
	1990	–	13	493	9	30
	1991	–	13	497	18	36
	1992	–	13	476	-	39
of which: non-EC countries	1975	56	27	1.242	–	-
	1980	55	28(a)	1.309	19	28
	1985	46	28	1.036	18	29(b)
	1986	–	30	1.048	18	-
	1987	47	32	1.074	18	-
	1988	49	35	1.104	17	-
	1989	56	34	1.163	15	26
	1990	–	34	1.247	14	33
	1991	–	35	1.346	12	40
	1992	–	33	1.491	-	129

Source: Eurostat

(a) 1981; (b) 1983; (c) 30.9; (d) including III.167 peopleof unknown nationality; (e) incl. 97.911 people of unknown nationality; (f) average 1966-1988; (g) 1987-1989; (h) 1989-1991.

Table 4.1:   *continued*

France	Ire-land	Italy	Luxem-bourg	Nether-lands	Portugal	United Kingdom
3.442	-	-	-	-	-	-
-	-	211(a)	96(a)	473	109(a)	1.682(a)
4.061	79	-	99	559	80	1.700
-	-	-	98	553	87	1.736
-	-	-	-	568	90	-
-	84	407(d)	-	592	94	1.852(f)
-	79	434(e)	-	624	101	1.894(g)
3.597	81	490	117	642	101	2.476(h)
-	88	781	115	692	108	2.429
1.860	-	-	-	-	-	-
-	-	79(a)	89(a)	168	-	712(a)
1.566	65	-	93	173	21	729
-	-	-	91	162	23	754
-	-	-	-	160	24	-
-	66	90	-	157	25	828(f)
-	62	100	-	160	27	879(g)
1.312	63	130	106	163	29	873(h)
-	69	149	103	169	29	782
1.582	-	-	-	-	-	-
-	-	132(a)	-	306	-	971(a)
2.495	14	-	6	386	59	971
-	-	-	7	391	64	982
-	-	-	-	408	66	-
-	17	206	-	435	69	1.025(f)
-	17	236	-	464	74	1.015(g)
2.285	18	361	11	479	72	1.603(h)
-	19	632	13	524	79	1.647
1.900	13	10	49	113	-	791
1.208(a)	-	-	-	190	26(a)	833(a)
1.260	20	57(b)	53	166	31	821
1.173	21	-	55	169	-	-
1.131	20	-	59	176	33	-
1.160	22	-	64	176	35	982
1.203	20	-	71	192	-	-
-	21	381	78	197	37	751
-	24	234	87	214	40	704
-	-	309	92	-	-	-
1.045	-	-	46	59	-	347
653(a)	-	-	-	84	-	406(a)
640	17	14(b)	50	76	7	398
590	16	-	52	88	-	-
569	16	-	56	83	8	-
568	18	-	61	85	10	410
579	16	-	67	88	-	-
-	16	50	74	90	8	347
-	19	44	81	92	8	333
-	-	45	87	-	-	-
855	-	-	3	55	-	444
555(a)	-	-	-	106	-	427(a)
620	4	43(b)	3	90	24	423
583	4	-	3	92	-	-
562	4	-	3	95	26	-
593	4	-	3	93	26	572
624	4	-	4	103	-	-
-	5	332	4	109	29	404
-	5	190	5	122	32	371
-	-	264	5	-	-	-

It can be seen that the employment of EC workers stagnated or even dropped. How can the generally declining migration of labour between the EC countries be explained? To tackle this question some theoretical considerations on the determinants of labour migration will be presented before we draw conclusions and sum up our findings.

Why Do Workers Migrate? Determinants of Labour Migration

Economic theory provides two hypotheses why workers move. According to integration theory,[3] the creation of a single market generates additional welfare effects by enabling labour to move to where it is most productive. The theory argues that a shift occurs from less productive to more productive jobs until marginal productivity and hence pay (for the same work) are in alignment within the area of integration. Prerequisites to this are, of course, that labour is mobile, that workers know about the job opportunities in other countries, that no other constraints on migration exist in the narrow sense – work permits, residence permits – as well as in the broader sense, such as recognition of qualifications, cultural differences, the living and housing conditions and language.

In contrast thereto, classical foreign trade theory assumes the immobility of labour between states. The differences in production factor endowment – mineral resources, capital, technology, labour – are balanced out by means of trade, which raises prosperity. Each country concentrates on producing those goods for which it has a comparative advantage over the others, that is, those which it can produce more cheaply (Heckscher–Ohlin theorem). According to this theory, trade relations induce a division of labour in line with the comparative production advantages between countries. From this standpoint, labour migration is unnecessary. Trade is a substitute for labour migration. Apart from that capital is more mobile than labour.

For a better understanding of the migration process it is helpful to discuss the mobility of labour between countries of different levels of economic development and of similar levels of industrialization.

An economically motivated potential for migration arises when varying levels of economic development exist between countries. More specifically, we can identify push factors in the emigration countries and pull factors in the immigration countries. Pull factors are the prospects of higher pay and the availability of jobs in the respective destination country. Push factors can be lack of employment prospects, unemployment or low income in the home country. If both respective factors are present in two countries, there is a potential for migration. Demand-pull and supply-push factors can be compared to battery poles: both are necessary to get started. But before migration actually can take place further conditions have to be met: transparency/ information and the lifting of barriers. The workers willing to move must be informed about the conditions in the receiving country, and this country must be accessible in terms of distance and legal entry (illegal migration left aside). In general, the ensuing flows are regulated by legislative and/or administrative procedures such as type of work permit or residence permit, which limit access and duration of stay. In the EU context the latter barriers no longer play a role, but cultural and language differences still exist and act as barriers to international mobility.

Up to the beginning of the 1970s, when there was a corresponding need for labour most European industrialized countries pursued a comparatively liberal policy towards immigrant labour. When the receiving country adopts such an immigration and employment policy and there is a pronounced difference between the levels of industrialization and employment as well as earning prospects in the receiving and sending countries, the influx from the less developed countries will obviously persist; in fact it will grow. Böhning called this the 'self-feeding process of migration'.[4] This self-feeding immigration is triggered by two factors. At the beginning of the immigration process, the foreign workers take on jobs that are already unattractive to nationals. After a certain period, they obtain jobs that indigenous workers leave for status or prestige reasons. As there is an abundance of foreign workers, more replace the former in the jobs that they now find 'socially undesirable'. The employment of foreigners, therefore, provides nationals with greater vertical mobility. On the other hand, another cause of self-feeding immigration is that foreign workers tend to fetch their families, friends and acquaintances to the country. As long as there are considerable wage disparities between the receiving country and the country of origin a push for migration will continue to exist. Generally this cannot even be excluded for a saturated labour market, as evidenced by the influx of emigrants from non-Member States or the economic refugees to the EC.

All the investigations conducted so far on (voluntary) migration indicate that a major determinant is the differential in economic development and hence earning opportunities. But the emigration push does not solely depend on the absolute differences between income levels in the country of origin and the target country. The relative level of pay in the country of origin is important as well. If the income is above the poverty line and reaches a socially acceptable level, the income threshold to emigrate is bound to be high, that is, the absolute earnings differential must be considerable to cause labour to move. Otherwise people tend to stay. The wage ratios between the richer EU countries in the North such as France and Germany and the poorer ones in the South are something like 4 to 1 and relatively few people migrate – even though it is now easy for EU nationals to work in other EU countries. There are of course other factors at play besides wages. For example, if future prospects are expected to improve in one's own country an emigration may less be considered.

The considerations just described will gain new relevance in relation to the opening of the borders with the Eastern European countries. Past migration experience has taught that significant numbers of people could move from Eastern Europe in search of work in the Community and other countries if they become free to do so. But if the restructuring process gains momentum and positive growth rates materialize, a move of wages toward a 'socially acceptable' level of income may get under way in those countries and diminish the pressure to migrate.

To sum up: labour migration between EC countries has not increased. The pressure to migrate for economic reasons is low between countries of similiar levels of development or if improvement of the standards of living in the home country can be expected. If in the course of the integration process an alignment of economic development and, therefore, pay is to be expected, then a major migration impulse – income differentials – further diminishes. How European economic integration developed and what has been its possible impact on migration is described in the following section.

HOW DID EUROPEAN INTEGRATION DEVELOP?

An assessment of the migration of labour between the EC Member States requires a closer look at the development of European economic integration since the EC's foundation. The discussion of the determinants of labour migration revealed that trade, income and employment opportunities are major factors for migration. Questions arise such as: 'How have trade and the international division of labour within the Community developed? Did trade substitute for migration? Are trends for the convergence of income or employment opportunities of the regions perceivable which reduced the pressure for migration between the EC countries?'.

The following indicators show the progress of integration: the trade links between the Member States, the development of gross national products and of the transborder financial transfers to offset regional differences, and the availability of jobs, or, rather the lack of them – unemployment.

Trade between Member Countries

A glance at Table 4.2 showing world trade relations indicates that reciprocal trade between the EC countries (intra-EC trade) increased consistently. From 1960 to 1973 trade between the six founding countries, as a proportion of overall trade, increased from 35 to 50 per cent. This share stagnated until the mid-1980s and then rose to 60 per cent by 1992.

Both periods of marked increase in intra-EC trade coincided with periods of relatively strong economic growth. During these periods trade obstacles were greatly reduced: by 1968 all customs duties between the Member States had been abolished and a customs union with a common external tariff had been set up. The second period of comparatively strong economic growth relates to the creation of the single European market: in 1987 the Single European Act came into force. The Act's main purpose was to lay down the legal requirements of the time schedule for the completion of the single market.

The relationship between trade and economic growth is not a one-

Table 4.2   Trade of EC economies, 1960–1990

Year	1960–67		1968–72		1973–79		1980–84		1985–90	
Country	World	Intra-EC	World	Intra-EC	World	Intra-EC	World	Intra-EC	World	Intra-EC
Belgium and Luxembourg	37.5	64.8	42.8	71.2	48.9	71.2	61.5	67.0	60.8	71.7
Denmark	27.0	52.3	23.4	46.7	25.3	48.2	29.1	49.1	26.7	50.8
Germany	15.9	44.8	17.6	50.9	20.4	50.3	24.8	50.5	24.9	53.1
Greece	12.7	50.6	12.7	53.4	17.6	47.3	19.5	48.1	20.8	60.5
Spain	8.1	47.8	9.2	44.4	11.2	41.3	14.4	39.3	14.4	56.0
France	11.0	45.8	12.5	57.2	16.6	55.0	18.9	53.9	18.6	61.9
Ireland	33.6	72.2	35.3	71.6	45.8	74.3	50.1	73.1	52.0	72.2
Italy	11.7	42.9	13.1	49.5	18.4	48.7	19.4	46.1	16.9	55.0
Netherlands	37.7	62.7	36.4	67.8	40.6	65.9	47.8	64.1	49.0	67.8
Portugal	19.8	48.3	20.3	49.6	22.2	50.2	30.1	50.1	32.5	65.1
United Kingdom	16.0	26.7	16.7	31.2	22.3	37.9	21.6	44.1	21.0	49.9
EC–12	8.8	45.0	8.3	51.9	10.2	52.6	11.5	52.2	9.8	59.8

Notes:

Figures for world trade as a % of GDP have been calculated by inserting country data for imports and exports of goods (SITC categories 0–9) in the formula:

$$\frac{\frac{1}{2}\sum(x+m) \times 100}{GDP}$$ Intra-EC trade is given as a % of total trade

For the Member States, figures for world trade as a % of GDP include intra-Community trade; for EC–12, intra-Community trade has been excluded.

Sources: Eurostat and Tsoukalis, Loukas: *The New European Economy*, Oxford University Press Inc, New York, 1993, p. 215.

way-street; rather, they influence each other. The favourable economic situation facilitated the rapid dismantling of internal customs duties and trade quotas between 1958 and 1968 and the setting up of the single market during the short time up to 1993. Fiercer international competition requires restructuring, which induces work and capital costs and makes manpower redundant.

In times of sound economic growth restructuring costs can be compensated for by means of better sales opportunities and the labour made redundant can be employed in newly created jobs. Therefore times of economic prosperity spur progress in economic integration. In this context Tsoukalis writes of a 'virtuous circle',[5] i.e. the coinciding of a number of favourable factors: a good economic climate, facilitating the acceptance of agreements to dismantle trade barriers; and liberalization, which, in turn, leads to more intensive trade and ultimately to more economic growth. Under poor economic conditions, competition-enhancing agreements are more difficult to achieve and the adjustment and restructuring processes required by a transition period are more painful, as redundancies are not offset by newly created jobs.

A number of studies showed that trade *within* industrial sectors and product groups (intra-industrial trade) grew more than between industrial sectors (inter-industrial trade) in the course of European integration. This indicates more (horizontal) specialization within the economic sectors, i.e. a diversification of the products within the sector rather than a division of labour in the form of production displacements. Production displacements would have led to adjustment problems such as the loss of whole production units and the associated redundancies.

The largely intra-industrial trade within the European Community is explained as follows:

> The existence of similar and therefore competitive, as opposed to complementary, production structures is clearly a necessary condition for intra-industry specialization to arise. If there is also some similarity of demand conditions among the member countries, reflected in overlapping tastes, and if goods are produced with economies of scale, so limiting the amount of product diversity that domestic producers can accommodate profitably, there will be an incentive to horizontal specialization within industries in order to benefit from the economies of

large-scale production.[6]

The situation has changed somewhat with the accession of other Mediterranean Member States to the Community. The EC is now divided into a north with a per capita gross domestic product (GDP) above the EC-average and a south – Greece, Portugal, Spain, Southern Italy, Ireland – with a below-average GDP per capita. This has tended to lay relatively more weight on inter-industry specialization associated with the exploitation of a comparative advantage. Such specialization may, in turn, be causing more adjustment problems than past integration.[7]

Trends of Gross National Product

The development of incomes across the Member States and the availability of jobs are further indicators of economic integration with relevance for migration movements. Migration of labour largely depends on differences in income between regions/countries and job opportunities.

In Table 4.3, as a proxy for income, the development of per capita gross national product in the 12 EC countries is shown in relation to the EC average. The table indicates that the per capita GDPs of the EC countries have converged. As a measure of this convergence the last line shows the divergence from the mean value (standard deviation). The decrease from 1960 (36.6) to 1993 (23.8) means less deviation from the EC average, or, in other words, a convergent development.

Such global average figures do, however, conceal differences between the regions within the EC countries. These differences can be considerable. In Italy the North/South gap is particularly obvious: Lombardy, in the North, has a per capita gross national product which is 37 per cent above the EC average, while that of Calabria in the South is 44 per cent below the EC average (1990). Differences between the highest and the lowest incomes in the regions of the Member States of similar magnitude also occur in other countries. For example, West Germany ranges from 83 per cent above average to 19 per cent below average; France, from 67 per cent above to 23 per cent below; the United Kingdom, from 54 per cent above to 23 per cent below; the

Table 4.3   Divergence of gross domestic product per capita 1960–1993
(EC countries, EC–12 = 100)

Country	1960	1970	1980	1990	1993
Belgium	97.5	101.1	106.4	104.9	106.2
Denmark	115.2	112.2	105.0	105.8	107.5
Germany	124.3	118.6	119.1	117.6	116.4
Greece	34.8	46.4	52.3	47.5	47.8
Spain	58.3	72.2	71.7	75.4	77.2
France	107.7	112.7	113.9	110.0	111.9
Ireland	57.2	56.1	60.2	69.0	71.6
Italy	86.6	95.5	102.5	102.8	104.0
Luxembourg	155.3	138.4	115.6	127.2	129.8
Netherlands	116.8	114.1	109.2	102.4	102.6
Portugal	37.2	46.9	52.7	53.7	58.1
United Kingdom	122.6	103.5	96.4	100.5	96.2
EC–12	100	100	100	100	100
Standard deviation	36.6	29.1	24.4	24.3	23.8
USA	182.5	158.4	146.0	139.0	136.7
Japan	54.1	88.8	96.5	112.7	118.1

Note: Per capita GDP is given at current market prices per head of population and in purchasing power parities. Estimation for 1993.

Source: Commission of the European Communities, *European Economy*, No. 54, Brussels, 1993, p. 206.

171

Netherlands from 34 per cent above to 37 per cent below; and Belgium, from 64 per cent above to 22 per cent below average.[8]

The differences between low-income and high-income regions persisted over time. Regional economic differences may become even more pronounced during the integration processes as the disappearance of trade impediments intensifies competition. Thus the already competitive countries and regions are strengthened, the competitively weak, mostly peripheral regions, fall even further behind. In order to offset regional differences, the European Regional Development Fund was set up in 1975. Its effect was insignificant, though, because insufficient funds were provided and were scattered over too many regions.

With the creation of the single European market the Commission of the European Communities became aware of the danger of the regions drifting apart and emphasized the necessity for counter measures in the White Paper on the completion of the single market.[9]

In 1988 various EC funds – Regional Fund, Agricultural Fund, Social Fund – were merged into the Structural Fund which was to concentrate on the less developed regions or on certain objectives such as combating youth unemployment or long-term unemployment. At the same time, the funds provided were considerably expanded. In 1992 they amounted to almost 20 billion ECU. By 1999 this amount is expected to have almost doubled. Thus the funds are no longer a *quantité négligeable*. In 1992, capital from the Structural Fund already made up 28 per cent of the EC Commission's budget and for countries such as Portugal, Greece or Ireland it meant several per cent of their national products.

Employment and Unemployment

In addition to the GDP, employment, or, rather a lack thereof – unemployment – is another major indicator of regional welfare. Table 4.4 shows annual employment growth for the EC, the USA and Japan. Compared to the United States and Japan overall employment grew only modestly in the EC, although at different speeds in the various countries. This modest increase in employment was not due to less economic growth. The EC's GDP growth was comparable to that of the United States over the last two decades. But in the EC the intensity of employment – the relative change in employment relating to a corresponding change in GDP was higher.

Table 4.4   *Average annual employment growth in EC countries, USA and Japan*

Country	1961–70	1971–80	1981–90	1991–93
Belgium	0.6	0.2	0.2	–0.6
Denmark	1.1	0.7	0.5	–0.8
Germany (West)	0.2	0.2	0.5	0.6
Greece	–0.8	0.7	1.0	–0.1
Spain	0.7	–0.6	0.8	–1.7
France	0.6	0.5	0.2	–0.6
Ireland	0.0	0.9	–0.2	0.4
Italy	–0.5	1.0	0.6	–1.0
Luxembourg	0.6	1.2	1.8	2.5
Netherlands	1.2	0.2	0.5	0.7
Portugal	0.4	–0.3	–0.4	–0.6
United Kingdom	0.2	0.2	0.5	–2.1
EC–12	0.3	0.3	0.5	–1.0
USA	1.9	2.0	1.9	0.2
Japan	1.4	0.7	1.1	1.1

Sources: Commission of the European Communities: (1) *European Economy* No. 58, Brussels, p. 119 and (2) *European Economy*, Supplement A, No. 11/12, Nov./Dec. 1994.

The Community's unemployment rate was 3.5 per cent in 1975. By 1985 the number of those out of work amounted to 15 million (EC–12), resulting in an unemployment rate of 10.8 per cent. The situation improved up to 1990 – 8.3 per cent – only to worsen afterwards. In 1992, the unemployment rate rose to 9.3 per cent. With the exception of Germany and Luxembourg, unemployment was more serious for the young and for women: in 1992 unemployment for young people amounted to 18.2 per cent and for women to 11.2 per cent.

The countries and regions of the Community are not affected evenly by unemployment. There are considerable differences between countries (Table 4.5). In general unemployment problems tend to exacerbate the inequalities in the GDP, although excessive generalization must be avoided. The regional pattern of unemployment does not follow a simple core-periphery model. Regions with traditional industries that were radically restructured or even eliminated during the 1970s and 1980s also suffered very high unemployment rates. The relatively high rates recorded in the northern-central UK as well as in areas like the West Midlands (12.4 per cent in 1987) are ample proof hereof. Elsewhere, patches of high unemployment can be found in the geographical centre of the Common Market in regions like the Nord-Pas-de-Calais in France (14 per cent) or Wallonie in Belgium (14.4 per cent).[10]

Table 4.5   *Unemployment rates in EC countries, USA and Japan (annual averages – Eurostat definition)*

Country	1971–80	1981–90	1991–93
Belgium	4.6	10.7	8.4
Denmark	3.7	7.6	9.6
Germany (West)	2.2	6.0	4.8
Greece	2.2	7.1	8.7
Spain	5.4	18.4	18.8
France	4.1	9.2	10.1
Ireland	7.7	15.7	17.5
Italy	6.1	9.7	10.5
Luxembourg	0.6	2.5	2.0
Netherlands	4.4	10.1	7.7
Portugal	5.1	7.0	4.3
United Kingdom	3.8	9.7	9.8
EC–12	4.2	9.6	9.7
USA	6.4	7.1	7.0
Japan	1.8	2.5	2.3

Sources: Commission of the European Communities: (1) *European Economy* No. 58, Brussels 1994, p. 120 and (2) *European Economy*, Supplement A, No. 11/12, Nov./Dec. 1994.

To sum up one can say that integration in the European Community is well advanced with regard to trade: trade relations between the Member

States intensified. Trade and competition happened less between the different sectors of industry than within such sectors or product groups. This is the result of the integration of countries with roughly comparable levels of economic development. Trade increased because of the specialization of products within industries rather than because of a division of labour in the form of production displacements. Production displacements would have ruined whole industrial units and caused mass redundancies. The ensuing unemployment would have been a potential incentive to migrate. In general this migration pressure did not come about.

Incomes, seen across the Member States in terms of the per capita national product, exhibit a convergent tendency, although considerable regional differences within the Member States still prevail. These persisting or even widening gaps between low-income and high-income regions within Member States tend to contain potential migration flows within individual Member States and not to induce workers to migrate across national borders. Employment, another indicator for welfare and a factor in migration, did not live up to expectations: overall employment growth remained modest and a continuous increase in unemployment can be observed.

Finally, it can be concluded that in the course of European integration trade has substituted for migration. The prosperity gap – a major factor for migration – has been mitigated by increased trade between the EC countries. Furthermore, capital is more mobile than labour and can substitute migration. Therefore, cross-border labour migration between EC countries has not increased.[11] Intra-industry trade, a characteristic feature of European integration, as mentioned earlier, entailed less risk of losing entire plants – and hence jobs – in favour of other countries. Migration thus did not complement trade relations between the EC countries.[12] Classical foreign trade theory is confirmed here. This, of course, does not rule out the emergence of occasional sectoral or qualification-related gaps between countries that then generate a migration potential.

This may result in movements of certain categories of workers, but not in large-scale migration.

WHAT TYPE OF MIGRATION IN THE EUROPEAN UNION?

Between the Countries of the European Union

Twenty years ago there was an influx of unskilled or semi-skilled migrant workers from outside the European Community into most Community Member States who balanced the dramatic labour shortage at the lower end of the labour market. However, employment and the demand for labour have changed radically since then: the number of vacancies for the least qualified workers is much lower; unemployment among them is disproportionately high. The presence of large numbers of unemployed nationals, both EC and third country nationals with low levels of skills, means that even if the demand for labour were to increase it could easily be met without immigration.

In addition, certain general conditions have changed. Owing to their declining demographic trends – apart from Ireland and Portugal – and continued industrialization, the outlying countries of the EC that have served so far as manpower reservoirs for the European industrialized nations will in future need more workers themselves. Some countries, such as Italy, Spain, or Greece, are already drawing large numbers from the labour force of third countries, particularly from Africa and Asia.[13] For example, 1 to 1.5 million foreigners are estimated to be living in Italy, mostly illegally. With the opening of the borders of the Central and Eastern European states, migration pressure will not only come from the developing countries but also from the Eastern countries.

As stated earlier, migration streams are strongly determined by different levels of income between the home country and the immigration country. But the emigration push does not solely depend on the absolute difference between income levels in the country of origin and the target country. The relative level of pay in the country of origin is important as well. If a certain income is perceived as socially acceptable at home the threshold triggering emigration will probably be higher, i.e. the absolute gap between earnings may widen without necessarily causing labour to migrate. The progressive industrialization of the peripheral countries of the EC levelled out economic development and pay rates in the EC countries. Thus the economic threshold for migration to another country may be crossed in only some sectors or skill levels.

'The dynamics of migration show that market forces – the conditions surrounding labour supply and demand, and the nature of economic growth – have had a greater impact than institutional factors, such as, in the case of the EC, the introduction of freedom of movement'.[14]

Based on the foregoing, it should be clear that, even after the completion of the single European market, there is no reason to expect spectacular migration of labour between current EC Member States. But partial imbalances for certain groups of workers may arise and additional, economically motivated migration could occur:

1.   *Such migration* might come about because specialists, managers, technicians and other highly qualified manpower will be in demand in all EC countries and are expected to move across borders more frequently. This is a consequence of the globalization and internationalization of companies. Data for the Federal Republic of Germany confirm the hypothesis of more migration of highly qualified manpower (Table 4.6). Whereas overall employment of EC nationals has gone down, employment of graduates from EC countries has risen almost throughout, although the level is still quite low. This phenomenon, incidentally, is not confined to the EC countries; it can be observed worldwide.[15]

A survey of multinational companies in the EC[16] commissioned by the Commission of the European Communities proves that 'Euro-executives' are more and more appreciated. These are either nationals with experience abroad or from another EC country. A stay abroad is increasingly considered desirable and supported by companies as one stage in a successful career. This practice of going abroad is bringing about a highly qualified, internationally mobile group that is linguistically, technically and culturally flexible. This group is still small in numbers, but its members will be increasingly in demand by companies acting internationally.

Table 4.6   *Foreign employees in the Federal Republic of Germany by occupational qualification 1977–1992 (indices 1980 = 100)*

Level of qualification	Foreign employees					
	total			EC nationals		
	1977	1987	1992	1977	1987	1992
Trainees	87	157	292	92	82	93
Employees with low qualification	96	74	94	103	62	60
Middle-level qualification	93	87	109	94	78	82
Graduate employees	86	98	122	84	96	115
Total employees	95	80	102	100	67	67
Absolute numbers (in 1.000)	1.889	1.589	2.036	730	492	494

Source: Employment Statistics (Bundesanstalt für Arbeit).

2.   *More migration* could also take place because regional economic areas near the borders will grow together even more. Certain Euro-regions might emerge in which national borders will increasingly forfeit their separating function. Commuting, whereby the place of residence and the place of work are in different countries might result and spread there. This is true, for instance, for the Franco-German border, where such commuting has increased.

Workers in border areas are particularly fast to react to changes in the neighbouring country. In addition, many of the obstacles which play a role in migration across borders, do not apply to these workers or are less important: normal surroundings, including housing, need not be changed, children can stay in the national school system, the spouse can keep his/her employment, language problems are relatively minor, because of the proximity of the border.

3.   *Temporary exchanges* in education and on-the-job training, study courses abroad, business travel and the like constitute a special type of migration. These will increase and they do not necessarily imply a permanent change of residence. Such stays abroad must not be recorded statistically and are therefore difficult to quantify. Nevertheless, it seems certain that they are increasing, because they are connected with the internationalization of business firms. They are a modern form of, or a substitute, for the traditional migration of labour.

A number of programmes of the Commission provide financial support for such exchanges.

4.   *Another type* of temporary immigration of labour is the current phenomenon of so-called contracted workers from EU-countries, mainly in constructon. Companies from another EU-country, normally one with low wages such as Portugal, are performing a constructon contract in Germany bringing along their cheap labour. The workers are not paid according to German bargained wage rates. The problem of undercutting local wages with cheaper EU contract workers (social dumping) was already recognized at the time of the discussion about the creation of the European internal markets and therefore it was proposed to pay these contract workers according to local wages at the place of performance. However, the Commission's corresponding draft directive has so far been blocked in the Council of Ministers.

The Big Question: The Future of Immigration from Eastern Europe and Third World Countries

In contrast to the EU countries, considerable differences exist in the level of development in comparison to the reform states of Central and Eastern Europe and the Third World countries. Therefore, a considerable migration presssure will continue to exist. Almost all Western European countries have experienced a dramatic surge in the number of people seeking asylum in recent years. In 1974, regular recruitment of foreign workers was drastically reduced in the wake of the oil-price shock and the poor labour market situation. Even today there is a more or less stringent freeze on hiring new foreign workers from outside the EU. Only reunification of families and certain exceptions were permitted, if the national labour market could not provide suitable labour. Access to the rich countries was only possible when applying for asylum or by staying illegally. The Geneva Convention for Refugees protects those who are suffering political persecution but not those attracted to the richer countries because of the economic plight of their home countries – the so-called economic refugees. Determining and verifying whether or not there is real political persecution in an individual case is difficult and takes time. Applicants rejected after many years are frequently allowed to stay for humanitarian reasons.[17]

If checks of people at the borders within the EU are abolished a uniform type of control at the external borders has to be established. Otherwise, economic refugees could gain access to the EU at the easiest point of entry and then apply for asylum in another country or reapply, if their original application had been rejected. This is why policies regarding visa and asylum must be uniform throughout the EU. Policies regarding immigrants and asylum-seekers are still, however, considered to be national affairs.

The transformations in Eastern Europe and the opening of the borders were political events of major significance. Compared to the Western industrial countries, the Central and Eastern European countries are poor. Their economies are not organized like those that evolved under the competitive conditions of free market economies. The service sector, for example, is underdeveloped and employment in agriculture cannot be maintained at previous levels. The manufacturing sector is often characterized by large conglomerates with low productivity, due to obsolete plant and equipment and labour hoarding. Restructuring and privatization will take time and money, neither of which these countries can afford.

For the time being, investment from outside will not be high enough to ensure rapid economic progress. Revenue from exports will be minor for some time, because low productivity and poor quality standards prevent them from being really competitive. Industries that might still be competitive – such as agriculture, textiles or steel – meet resistance when demanding the opening of the EU markets. The counterparts of these industries in the EU are either subsidized or are themselves in trouble.

At any rate, declining output and high unemployment can be expected in the course of the restructuring process. Table 4.7 shows the output and unemployment trends for the European transition economies. After heavy output losses up to 1993 moderate increases are expected for most countries in the future. But with the exception of the Czech Republic, unemployment will remain high. For lack of funds, unemployment benefit will not be any compensation for wages lost during the foreseeable period of mass unemployment.

Table 4.7   *Output and unemployment in Central and Eastern*
European transition countries (output as GDP
percentage change over previous year and unemployment
as percentage of labour force)

Country	1992	1993	1994	1995
Bulgaria				
Output	−7.1	−4.0	0	0
Unemployment	15.2	16.3	17	17
Czech Republic				
Output	−6.6	−0.3	2	5
Unemployment	2.6	3.5	5	7
Hungary				
Output	−5.0	−1.0	1	2
Unemployment	12.3	12.2	11	11
Poland				
Output	2.6	4.0	4	3
Unemployment	13.6	15.7	16	15
Romania				
Output	−15.4	1.0	0	1
Unemployment	8.4	10.2	13	15
Russia				
Output	−19.0	−12.0	−10	−2
Unemployment	−	−	−	−
Slovak Republic				
Output	−7.0	−4.1	0	2
Unemployment	10.4	14.4	16	16

Source: OECD: Economic Outlook, June 1994, Paris, p. 115, 118.

Therefore these countries will experience strong pressure for emigration. This potential to migrate is – in contrast to Third World countries – not backed up by demographic trends. There is no fundamental difference between the demographic situation of the countries of Central and Eastern Europe and that of European OECD countries.[18] Thus the incentive to migrate is primarily provided by differences in living standards between emigration and immigration areas and by the availability of employment opportunities in the EU countries.

But the current situation is different from the 1960s and early 1970s when Central European countries recruited large numbers of low-skilled foreign workers. At that time unskilled or semi-skilled migrant workers offset the great shortages at the lower end of the labour market, predominantly in manufacturing and construction. Now the manufacturing sector is shrinking in terms of the numbers of employed. Moreover, there is no demand for low-skilled workers.

In contrast to typical immigration countries, such as the USA, EU governments have no positive 'ideology' towards permanent immigration. In principle, the immigration stop for new foreign workers imposed in EC countries in 1974 is still in force. Policies on admission for employment of new foreign workers have been restrictive. If anything, these policies have become more restrictive, due to the significant increase in unemployment throughout the European Union.[19]

To alleviate the pressure to migrate, and at the same time to help those countries in their restructuring process, proposals were made to allow more temporary migration for seasonal work, project-tied work[20] and for training. By opening various revolving doors for migration, illegal employment of foreign workers is supposed to be reduced and the migration flow to be channelled. For the time being, only Germany has opened various legal opportunities for temporary migrants on a larger scale by concluding bilateral agreements with a number of Central and Eastern European states.[21] In 1993, 181,000 seasonal workers and 70,000 project workers from transition economies were employed.

It was thus hoped to avoid a substantial and unauthorized influx of foreign workers with the unwanted effects of exploitation and marginalization of those workers or to avoid wage-dumping. With more or less open borders, illegal migration and employment cannot be ruled out completely. But the much feared massive and uncontrollable influx of migrants from the East did not occur. There is considerable migration, however, between and inside these countries.[22] If a pressure to migrate materializes or not depends, among other things, on whether the people perceive any improvement in the near future in their own countries. The figures presented in Table 4.7 give room for this hope, at least for some countries, in particular for the Czech Republic, Hungary and also for Poland. For Bulgaria, Romania, the Slovak Republic and Russia the economic situation will remain very difficult for the foreseeable future.

THE OUTLINE OF A EUROPEAN IMMIGRATION POLICY?

Immigration pressure from third countries will persist in the future as well, both from the reform countries in Eastern Europe and from the Third World. After the border controls within the European Union have been abolished, a uniform migration policy will be required. As stated above, there is the problem that third country nationals might look for the 'softest spot', i.e. the easiest point of entry and then migrate to other countries within the Union. Another problem is the different treatment of third country nationals who have already been residing legally in a member country and want to work in another EU country. Should they also enjoy freedom of movement and if so under what conditions? So far, this is not the case. Free movement of labour only applies to EU nationals. This results in different treatment of third country nationals in the case of cross-border migration. Also the conditions for obtaining nationality are very different in the various member countries. Non-EU nationals living in a country where nationality is relatively easily awarded might obtain the nationality of that EU country after a short while and then be eligible for free movement of labour.

In the Treaty on the European Union the Member States agreed to consider asylum policy, the regulations for crossing the borders to third countries, immigration policy and their policy regarding third country nationals as 'Matters of Common Interest'.[23] This means that these policy issues will continue to be dealt with by cooperation between governments and not as policy of the Union. However, this cooperation has now been formalized as the Commission, the Council, the European Parliament and possibly the European Court of Justice become involved to ensure coherence of Community actions.[24] Just as the

Member States, the Commission is entitled to initiate legislation and is extensively involved in all work being done on asylum and immigration policy.

However, for the limited field of a compulsory visa, and the uniform design of such a visa, for third country nationals the first step towards 'supra-nationality' has already been taken: article 100c of the EU Treaty provides that the Council shall determine the countries 'whose nationals must possess a visa when entering a Member State from a third country'. The decision must for the time being be taken unanimously and after 1 January 1996 with a qualified majority.

The EC Commission has meanwhile explained the framework for the immigration and asylum policies of the Union in a document.[25] This 'Communication from the Commission to the Council and the European Parliament' consists of three parts:

1. Dealing with root causes of migration pressure

The Commission argues that such action 'requires ensuring that immigration and asylum policies are fully integrated into the Union's external policies, and that the various external policy instruments available to the Union are used to address the root causes of those pressures'. That could involve action at a number of different levels such as in the areas of trade, development and cooperation policies, humanitarian assistance and human rights policies.[26]

2. Controlling migration flows

The prevailing concept of this part is the necessity to harmonize immigration and asylum policies. The 'control' should not necessarily imply bringing migration flows to an end, but to manage them. 'Defining grounds for admission in clear terms makes it possible to translate those concepts into practical policies'.[27] Special mention is made of family reunion, common standards for asylum proceedings, granting residence/work permits for foreign workers and self-employed and treatment of illegal immigrants.

Regarding the influx of labour from third countries the Commission remains rather reserved. It states:

With the present economic and labour market situation these admission policies will generally have to remain of a restrictive nature in the short term. ... the setting of quotas, a measure which has been suggested as a means to alleviate the migration pressure, does not correspond with the existing economic situation in the short run. The longer term approach to the issue of labour-related migration will also of necessity have to take account of developments in the economic and labour market situation ... Irrespective of the outcome of such a general analysis, there are good reasons to refrain from applying restrictive policies in case of temporary work schemes [supposedly, what is meant are work contracts limited in time] and seasonal and frontier workers.[28]

3. Strengthening integration policies for the benefit of legal immigrants

In the view of the Commission any successful integration policy includes

security of stay and permanent residence for all those satisfying stability criteria. Without this foundation, uncertainty will pervade other aspects of the integration process (such as family reunification, access to employment, housing, health, education and training). ... Special attention also needs to be given to the residence status of members of the family of legally resident immigrants ... Children or grandchildren of immigrants who have not become nationals of the Member State in which they live but who themselves have been resident in the Member State for an appropriate qualifying period should be able to enjoy security of status when they are above school age. Similarly, foreign-born spouses of established immigrants or nationals should enjoy independent residence rights after a qualifying period.[29]

The Commission goes on to stress that

the logic of the internal market implied the elimination of the condition of nationality for the exercise of certain rights. A first step in this respect would be to enable third country nationals to move freely around within the Union on the basis of their residence permit, which would replace any existing visa requirement. ... as far as the crossing of external frontiers is concerned it has proposed giving residence permits of third country nationals the equivalent value to a visa. ... another consideration is free movement for the purpose of engaging in an economic activity ... a first step towards improvement in this area would be for Member States to accord priority to third-country nationals permanently and legally resident in another Member State, when job vacancies cannot be filled by EU-nationals. Allowing such third country nationals access to employment in another Member State in response to an offer of employment would represent a further step.[30]

The situation of self-employed persons seeking the right of establishment in another Member State would also need to be addressed.[31]

This chapter can be summarized as follows: the Communication from the Commission to the Council and the European Parliament on Immigration and Asylum Policies was the first attempt to define the general outlines of a union-wide immigration policy. However, this does not mean that there are already any common immigration and asylum policies in the Union. Many of the proposals are rather vague and still require extensive consultation and harmonization. So far, immigration policy has been regarded as a national domain. Even the Maastricht Treaty does no more than mention the harmonization of the conditions for granting and the design of visas for third country nationals as matters of Union law. The remaining important matters continue to be dealt with in the form of cooperation between governments – albeit in the institutional framework of the EU. Presently the Member States' regulations and interests are too diverse to expect a comprehensive common immigration policy in the near future.[32] Only after several partial fields have been harmonized and authority has been transferred to the Commission, will a uniform migration policy throughout the European Union emerge.

NOTES

1   Free movement of labour in the EEC Treaty means the 'abolition of any discrimination based on nationality between workers of the Member States as regards employment, remuneration and other conditions of work and employment'.
2   Cf. R. Penninx and P. Muus, 'No limits for migration after 1992? The lessons of the past and a reconnaissance of the future', *International Migration*, No. 3/1989, p. 373 and Heinz Werner, 'Freizügigkeit der Arbeitskräfte und die Wanderungsbewegungen in den Ländern der Europäischen Gemeinschaft'

(Free Movement of Labour and Migration Flows in the Countries of the European Community), *Mitteilungen aus der Arbeitsmarkt- und Berufs-forschung* 4/1973, p. 339.

3   Robson, Peter, *The Economics of International Integration*, London, 1987, p. 65; Thomas Straubhaar, 'Labour Migration within a Common Market: Some aspects of EC experience', *Journal of Common Market Studies*, September 1988, p. 46; George Borjas, 'Economic theory and international migration', *International Migration Review*, No. 3/1989, pp. 457 ff.

4   Böhning, W.R., *Studies in International Labour Migration*, London and Basingstoke, 1984, pp. 68 ff.

5   Tsoukalis, Loukas, *The New European Economy*, Oxford University Press, 1993, p. 29.

6   Robson, Peter, *The Economics of International Integration*, Unwin Hyman Ltd., London, 1987, p. 42.

7   Sapir, André, *Regional Integration in Europe*, Commission of the European Communities, Economic Papers No. 94, Brussels, 1991, p. 11.

8   Figures are taken from Regio, the databank of the Commission of the European Communities. Purchasing power parities are calculated which express the price of an identical volume of goods and services for each country to allow comparisons between regions.

9   'EC Integration, by increasing the possibility for human, material and financial resources to move without hindrance toward the most economically attractive regions, could lead to an increase in regional disparities', Commission of the European Communities, *Completing the Internal Market*, White Paper from the Commission to the European Council, Luxembourg, 1985, p. 8.

10 Figures refer to 1987 and are taken from Wise, Mark and Gibb, Richard, *Single Market to Social Europe*, John Wiley & Sons, Inc., New York, 1993, p. 208.

11 The mobility of labour amongst EC countries thus declined along with the regional mobility within the EC countries. Cf. Karr, W., Koller, M., Kridde, W., Werner, H., 'Regionale Mobilität am Arbeitsmarkt' (Regional Mobility on the Labour Market), *Mitteilungen aus der Arbeitsmarkt- und Berufsforschung*, No. 2/1987, pp. 197 ff.

12 Straubhaar, Thomas, *On the Economics of International Labour Migration*, Bern and Stuttgart, 1988, pp. 127 ff.

13 Cf. OECD, SOPEMI – reports (continuous reporting system on migration), Paris, annual reports.

14 Tapinos, George, 'Regional economic integration and its effects on employment and migration', in OECD, *Migration and Development*, Paris, 1994, p. 220.

15 Salt, John and Findlay, Allan, 'International migration of highly skilled manpower. Theoretical and development issues', in OECD, (Development Centre) *The Impact of International Migration on Developing Countries*, Paris, 1989, pp. 159 ff.; Findlay, Allan, 'New technology, high-level labour

movements and the concept of the brain drain', in OECD, *The Changing Course of International Labour Migration*, Paris 1993, pp. 149 ff. ; Stalker, Peter, *The Work of Strangers: a Survey of International Labour Migration*, International Labour Office, Geneva, 1994, S. 36 ff.

16   Walwei, Ulrich, Werner, Heinz, 'Europeanizing the labour market: Employee mobility and company recruiting methods', *Intereconomics*, January/February 1993, pp. 3–10.

17   In the Federal Republic of Germany 440,000 persons applied for political asylum in 1992. Even if their applications are rejected many of them are 'tolerated' to stay.

18   OECD, SOPEMI – *Trends in International Migration*, Paris, 1994, p. 109.

19   Commission of the European Communities, 'Communication from the Commission to the Council and the European Parliament on Immigration and Asylum Policies', COM(94) 23 final, Brussels, 23 February 1994, p. 9.

20   Project workers/workers on a contract for services are foreign workers who are seconded by their employer from the country of origin and who may be employed temporarily in another State for the purposes of a contract for services or the execution of a project.

21   Council of Europe, 'Agreements providing for short-term migration for employment and training purposes', Document MG-R-MT (94) 1, prepared by Heinz Werner for the Council of Europe, Strasbourg 1994.

22   Cf. OECD, SOPEMI, annual reports, op.cit.

23   Title VI, article K.1 of the 'Provisions on Cooperation in the Fields of Law and Internal Matters of the Treaty on the Foundation of the European Union'.

24   Brinkmann, G., 'Europäische Einwanderungspolitik' (European Immigration Policy), *Forschungsinstitut der Friedrich-Ebert-Stiftung – Gesprächskreis Arbeit und Soziales*, No. 32, 'Von der Ausländer- zur Einwanderungspolitik' (Moving from Aliens' Policy to Immigration Policy), Bonn, 1994, p. 117.

25   Commission of the European Communities, 'On Immigration and Asylum Policies', Communication from the Commission to the Council and the European Parliament, Brussels, 23 February 1994.

26   Commission of the European Communities, 'On Immigration and Asylum Policies', op.cit, p. 6.

27   Commission of the European Communities, 'On Immigration and Asylum Policies', op.cit, p. 20.

28   Commission of the European Communities, 'On Immigration and Asylum Policies', op.cit, pp. 21/22.

29   Commission of the European Communities, 'On Immigration and Asylum Policies', op.cit, p. 33.

30   Recently the European Court of Justice ruled in a very interesting case relating to the employment of third country nationals employed under a work contract by a company having its seat in the Union which sent them to work in another Member State: a Belgian demolition company (Vander Elst) worked on a one-month contract in France with Moroccan workers possessing a Belgian work

permit. The French authorities fined the Belgian company a substantial sum, because the Moroccan workers did not have a French work permit. The European Court of Justice held that the fine was illegal, because the facts involved rendering a service which may be offered and rendered also in another Member State under the concept of the internal market, including with workers from non-Member States (see Migration News Sheet, Brussels, September 1994, No. 138/94 –09, p. 1).

31   Commission of the European Communities, 'On Immigration and Asylum Policies', op.cit, p. 34.
32   Collinson, S., 'Towards further harmonization? Migration policy in the European Union', in *Studi Emigrazione*, XXXI (114), 1994, p. 236.

REFERENCES

Appleyard, Reginald (1991), *International Migration: Challenge for the Nineties*, Geneva, International Organization for Migration.

Ardittis, Solon (ed.) (1994), *The Politics of East–West Migration*, Houndmills, Basingstoke, Hampshire and London, Macmillan Press Ltd.

Böhning, W.R. (1984), *Studies in International Labour Migration*, London and Basingstoke, Macmillan Press Ltd.

Borjas, George (1989), 'Economic theory and international migration', *International Migration Review*, No. 3, pp. 457 ff.

Borjas, George and Richard Freeman (eds) (1992), *Immigration and the Work Force. Economic consequences for the United States and Source Areas*, National Bureau of Economic Research, Chicago and London: The University of Chicago Press.

Borrmann, Axel and Koopmann, Georg (1994), 'Regionalisation and regionalism in world trade', *Intereconomics*, July/August, pp. 163-70.

Brinkmann, Gisbert (1994), 'Europäische Einwanderungspolitik'. *Forschungsinstitut der Friedrich-Ebert-Stiftung – Gesprächskreis Arbeit und Soziales*, No. 32, Von der Ausländer- zur Einwanderungspolitik, Bonn, p. 117.

Castles, Stephen and Miller, Mark J. (1993), *The Age of Migration. International Population Movements in the Modern World*,

Houndmills, Basingstoke, Hampshire and London, Macmillan Press Ltd.

Center for Migration Studies (1989), 'International migration: an assessment for the '90s', Special silver anniversary issue, *International Migration Review*, No. 3.

Collinson, Sarah (1993a), *Europe and International Migration*, London and New York: Pinter Publishers for Royal Institute of International Affairs, London.

Collinson, Sarah (1993b), *Beyond Borders: West European Migration Policy Towards the 21st century*, London: Royal Institute of International Affairs.

Collinson, Sarah (1994), 'Towards further harmonization? Migration policy in the European Union', *Studi Emigrazione*, XXXI, (114), p. 236.

Commission des Communautés Européennes (1990), 'Dimension européenne de la gestion des ressources humaines dans les firmes multinationales', Doc.nr.V/1678/FR, Bruxelles.

Commission of the European Communities (1994), 'Communication from the Commission to the Council and the European Parliament on Immigration and Asylum Policies', COM(94) 23 final, Brussels, 23 February, p. 9.

Commission for the Study of International Migration and Cooperative Economic Development (1990), *Unauthorized Migration: An Economic Development Response*, Report, Washington: US Government Printing Office.

Council of Europe (1994), *Recent Demographic Developments in Europe 1993*, Strasbourg.

Eurostat (1993), Regionen – *Statistisches Jahrbuch*, Luxembourg.

Findlay, Allan (1993), 'New technology, high-level labour movements and the concept of the brain drain', in OECD, *The Changing Course of International Labour Migration*, Paris, pp. 149 ff.

Fisch, Gerhard (1994), 'Raumwirtschaftliche Aspekte der Kohäsionspolitik vor dem Hintergrund neuer Außen-handels-theorien', *Raumforschung und Raumordnung*, Heft 4/5, p. 255.

Friedrich-Ebert-Stiftung (1994), *Von der Ausländer- zur Einwandungs-politik. Forschungsinstitut der Friedrich-Ebert-Stiftung - Gesprächskreis Arbeit und Soziales*, No. 32, Bonn.

Giersch, Herbert (ed.) (1994), *Economic Aspects of International Migration*, Berlin, Heidelberg, New York, London, Paris, Tokyo, Springer.

Greenaway, David and Hine, Robert (1991), 'Intra-industry specialization, trade expansion and adjustment in the European Economic Space', *Journal of Common Market Studies*, No. 6, pp. 603–22.

Hammar, Tomas (ed.) (1985), *European Immigration Policy – A Comparative Study*, Cambridge, London, New York, New Rochelle, Melbourne, Sydney, Cambridge University Press.

Hof, Bernd (1993), *Europa im Zeichen der Migration – Szenarien zur Bevölkerungs- und Arbeitsmarktentwicklung in der Europäischen Gemeinschaft bis 2020*, Cologne: Deutscher Instituts-Verlag.

Hönekopp, Elmar (1991), 'Migratory movements from countries of Central and Eastern Europe: causes and characteristics, present situation and possible future trends – the cases of Germany and Austria', Council of Europe, Conference of Ministers on the movement of persons coming from Central and Eastern European countries, Vienna, 24–25 January 1991.

ILO (1992), *Migration*, Geneva.

International Organization for Migration (1992), 'Migration and Development', *International Migration*, XXX (3/4), special issue, Geneva.

Karr, W., Koller, M., Kridde, W., Werner, H. (1987), 'Regionale Mobilität am Arbeitsmarkt' (Regional Mobility on the Labour Market), *Mitteilungen aus der Arbeitsmarkt- und Berufsforschung*, No. 2, pp. 197 ff.

King, Russell (ed.) (1993a), *The New Geography of European Migrations*, London: Belhaven.

King, Russell (ed.) (1993b), *Mass Migration in Europe: The Legacy and the Future*, London: Belhaven.

Kommission der Europäischen Gemeinschaften (1985), *Vollendung des Binnenmarktes – Weißbuch der Kommission an den Europäischen Rat*, Brussels.

Kommission der Europäischen Gemeinschaften (1991), *Die Regionen in den 90er Jahren*, Brussels, Luxembourg.

Kommission der Europäischen Gemeinschaften (1993a), 'Die Zukunft der Gemeinschaftinitiativen im Rahmen der Strukturfonds', KOM(93) 282 endg., Brussels, 16 June 1993.

Kommission der Europäischen Gemeinschaften (1993b), *Strukturfonds der Gemeinschaft 1994–1999. Verordnungstexte und Erläuterungen*, Brussels, Luxembourg.

Kommission der Europäischen Gemeinschaften (1993c), *Dritter Jahres-bericht über die Durchführung der Strukturfonds – 1991*, Brussels, Luxembourg.

Kommission der Europäischen Gemeinschaften (1993d), 'Vierter Jahresbericht der Kommission über die Durchführung der Strukturfondsreform – 1992', KOM(93) 530 endg., Brussels, 29 October 1993.

Kritz, L. and H. Zlotnik (eds) (1992), *International Migration Systems: A Global Approach*, Oxford: Clarendon Press.

Martin, Philip L. (1993), *Trade and Migration: NAFTA and Agriculture*, Policy Analyses in International Economics, No. 38, Washington: Institute for International Economics.

Miles, Robert and Dietrich Thränhardt (eds) (1995), *Migration and European Integration. The Dynamics of Inclusion and Exclusion*, London: Pinter Publishers.

OECD (1987), *The Future of Migration*, Paris.

OECD (1993), *The Changing Course of International Migration*, Paris.

OECD (1994), *Migration and Development - New Partnerships for Co-operation*, Paris.

OECD, SOPEMI – *Trends in International Migration*,Various years, Paris.

Ohly, Claudia (1993), *What Have We Learned About the Economic Effects of EC Integration? A Survey of the Literature*, Commission of the European Communities, Economic Papers No. 103, Brussels.

Penninx, R. and Muus, P. (1989), 'No limits for migration after 1992? The lessons of the past and a reconnaissance of the future', *International Migration*, No. 3, p. 373.

Robson, Peter (1987), *The Economics of International Integration*, London: Unwin Hyman Ltd.

Rudolph, Hedwig and Mirjana Morokvasic (eds) (1993), *Bridging States and Markets: International Migration in the Early 1990s*, WZB, Berlin: edition sigma, Rainer Bohn Verlag.

Russell, Sharon Stanton and Teitelbaum, Michael S. (1992), *International Migration and International Trade*, World Bank Discussion Papers, No. 160, Washington.

Salt, John and Findlay, Allan (1989), 'International migration of highly skilled manpower: theoretical and development issues', in OECD (Development Centre), *The Iimpact of International Migration on Developing Countries*, Paris, pp. 159 ff.

Sapir, André (1992), *Regional Integration in Europe*, Commission of the European Communities, Economic Papers No. 94, Brussels.

Simon, Julian (1989), *The Economic Consequences of Immigration*, Oxford, Basil Blackwell Ltd.

Stalker, Peter (1994), *The Work of Strangers: A Survey of International Labour Migration*, Geneva: International Labour Office.

Straubhaar, Thomas (1988a), 'Labour Migration within a Common Market: Some aspects of EC experience', *Journal of Common Market Studies*, September, p. 46.

Straubhaar, Thomas (1988b), *On the Economics of International Labour Migration*, Bern and Stuttgart, Paul Haupt.

Swann, Dennis (1992), *The Economics of the Common Market*, Seventh edition, London, Penguin Books.

Tsoukalis, Loukas (1993), *The New European Economy*, New York, Oxford University Press.

United Nations (1994), 'Population Distribution and Migration', Proceedings of the United Nations Expert Meeting on Population Distribution and Migration, Santa Cruz, Bolivia, 18–22 January 1993 (convened in preparation for the International Conference on Population and Development, Cairo, 5–14 September 1994).

Walwei, Ulrich and Werner, Heinz (1992), 'Europäische Integration: Konsequenzen für Arbeitsmarkt und Soziales', *Mitteilungen aus der Arbeitsmarkt- und Berufsforschung* 4, pp. 483–98.

Walwei, Ulrich and Werner, Heinz (1993) 'Europeanizing the labour market: Employee mobility and company recruiting methods', *Intereconomics*, January/February, pp. 3–10.

Waniek, Roland (1994), 'EG-Regionalpolitik für die Jahre 1994 bis 1999', *Wirtschaftsdienst* No. 1, pp. 43–9.

Weidenfeld, Werner (ed.) (1993), *Der vollendete Binnenmarkt – eine Herausforderung für die Europäische Gemeinschaft. Strategien und Optionen für die Zukunft Europas*, Arbeitspapiere 11, Gütersloh: Bertelsmann Stiftung.

Werner, Heinz (1973), 'Freizügigkeit der Arbeitskräfte und die Wanderungsbewegungen in den Ländern der Europäischen Gemeinschaft', *Mitteilungen aus der Arbeitsmarkt- und Berufsforschung* 4, p. 339.

Werner, Heinz (1994a), 'Regional economic integration and migration: the European case', *The Annals of the American Academy of Political and Social Science*, 534, July, pp. 147–64.

Werner, Heinz (1994b), 'Agreements providing for short-term migration for employment and training purposes', Document MG-R-MT (94) 1, Council of Europe, Strasbourg.

Werner, Heinz (1994c), *Integration of foreign workers into the labour market – France, Germany, the Netherlands and Sweden*, International Labour Office, World Employment Programme, Working Paper, Geneva.

Werner, Heinz and Walwei, Ulrich (1992), 'Zur Freizügigkeit für Arbeitskräfte in der EG', *Mitteilungen aus der Arbeitsmarkt- und Berufsforschung* 1, pp. 1–12.

Wise, Mark and Gibb, Richard (1993), *Single Market to Social Europe*, New York: John Wiley & Sons, Inc.

Index

Abella, M. 100
Adams, R.H. 102
admission, circumstances of 123–33
Africa 15, 133
  skill migration 94–5
African slave migrations 18–23
Amin, B.A. 91
Anderson, A. 149
Argentina 60
Asch, B.J. 124, 130
Asia 15, 132–3
asylum-seekers 127
  EU 179–80, 188
  see also refugees
Athukorala, P. 89
Australia 43, 136–7, 150
  immigration and economic growth
    58–9
  immigration policy 130–1
Avina, J. 142
Awny, E. 91
Azam, F-I. 105

Baines, D. 7, 36, 37, 39, 40, 41
  European long-distance migration 32,
    33
Barth, G. 28
Bean, C.R. 146
Becker, G.S. 121
Beijer, G. 32
Belgium 162
Bilgrami, N. 101
Birrell, R. 131
black American population 139–45
Bodnar, J. 42
Bogen, E. 142, 143
Bohning, W.R. 129, 137, 145, 165, 187
border areas 178
Borjas, G. 3, 135, 149, 187
Bound, J. 138
Bouvier, L. 142
bracero programme 56–7

brain drain 55, 65, 93–4
  compensation proposals 109
  see also skill migration
'brain overflow' 94
Briggs, V.M. 123, 134, 135, 136, 142
  US immigration policy 125–6
Brimelow, P. 132
Brinkmann, G. 188
Britain *see* United Kingdom

Canada 57–8, 124, 134, 146, 149, 150
  equity 145
  immigration policy 127–8, 136
Caribbean 70
  slavery 18–19, 22
Castillo, M.A. 101
Castles, S. 66, 129
  migration as development aid 54
  postwar migrations 43, 53, 58, 59, 61
  transatlantic migration 36
Center for Immigration Studies 128, 131
Central/Eastern Europe 179–83
chain migration 41–3
China 87
Chinese coolie migrations 25, 26–7,
    27–8
Chiswick, B. 135
Choucri, N. 99
cities 10–11, 12, 117
Civil Rights Movement 140–1
classical theories of migration 83
Clayton, M. 128
Clout, H.D. 47
Cohen, R. 48
Collinson, S. 189
colonialism 16–31
  coolie migration 17, 23–31
  settlers 16–17
  slave migration 17–23
Commission of the European
    Communities 171, 173, 174, 188,
    188–9